MIND-SETS AND MISSILES:
A FIRST HAND ACCOUNT OF THE CUBAN
MISSILE CRISIS

Kenneth Michael Absher

August 2009

The views expressed in this report are those of the author and do not necessarily reflect the official policy or position of the Department of the Army, the Department of Defense, or the U.S. Government. Authors of Strategic Studies Institute (SSI) publications enjoy full academic freedom, provided they do not disclose classified information, jeopardize operations security, or misrepresent official U.S. policy. Such academic freedom empowers them to offer new and sometimes controversial perspectives in the interest of furthering debate on key issues.

*****

*****

I am indebted to Ambassador David Abshire, former U.S. Ambassador to NATO, for his encouragement and interest in the importance of identifying and understanding the role of mindsets in the analysis of foreign intelligence and the formation and implementation of foreign policy. As the first Research Fellow with the Scowcroft Institute at the George Bush School of Government and Public Service, I am indebted to Brent Scowcroft for the privilege of serving in his institute. I thank Dr. Jeff Engel, the Director of the Scowcroft Institute, and Dr. Joe Cerami of the Bush School for their encouragement and support. I thank Dr. Sam Kirkpatrick, former President of the University of Texas at San Antonio (UTSA), and Denis Clift, President of the National Defense Intelligence College (NDIC), for the privilege of teaching as an Adjunct Professor at UTSA from 1994 to 1997 and at NDIC from 1997 to 2002. I am also very much indebted to Dr. David Robarge, the Chief Historian at the Central Intelligence Agency's Center for the Study of Intelligence, who is an acknowledged expert on the Cuban Missile Crisis, for his encouragement and his excellent editorial guidance and wisdom. Finally, I am indebted to Dr. Sherman Kent for the privilege of serving in the Office of National Estimates during this historic crisis of the Cold War.

*****

This manuscript is lovingly dedicated to my wife, Cindy, whose constant love and support enabled me to continue researching and writing this paper over a period of many years.

*****

Comments pertaining to this report are invited and should be forwarded to: Director, Strategic Studies Institute, U.S. Army War College, 122 Forbes Ave, Carlisle, PA 17013-5244.

*****

All Strategic Studies Institute (SSI) publications are available on the SSI homepage for electronic dissemination. Hard copies of this report also may be ordered from our homepage. SSI's homepage address is: *www.StrategicStudiesInstitute.army.mil.*

*****

The Strategic Studies Institute publishes a monthly e-mail newsletter to update the national security community on the research of our analysts, recent and forthcoming publications, and upcoming conferences sponsored by the Institute. Each newsletter also provides a strategic commentary by one of our research analysts. If you are interested in receiving this newsletter, please subscribe on our homepage at *www.StrategicStudiesInstitute.army. mil/newsletter/.*

ISBN 1-58487-400-7

TABLE OF CONTENTS

FOREWORD

This Letort Paper provides a detailed chronology and analysis of the intelligence failures and successes of the Cuban Missile Crisis. The author, Mr. Kenneth Absher, contends that, when our national security is at stake, the United States should not hesitate to undertake risky intelligence collection operations, including espionage, to penetrate our adversary's deceptions. At the same time, the United States must also understand that our adversary may not believe the gravity of our policy warnings or may not allow its own agenda to be influenced by U.S. diplomatic pressure.

As both a student of and key participant in the events of the crisis, the author is able to provide in-depth analysis of the failures and successes of the national intelligence community and executive leadership during the buildup to the confrontation, and the risky but successful actions which led to its peaceful settlement. From his analysis, the author suggests considerations relevant to the collection, analysis, and use of intelligence which have continuing application.

DOUGLAS C. LOVELACE, JR.
Director
Strategic Studies Institute

SUMMARY

This Letort Paper provides a detailed chronology and analysis of the intelligence failures and successes of the Cuban Missile Crisis, and suggests the applicability of lessons learned to the collection, analysis, and use of intelligence in strategic decisionmaking. The author was assigned to Sherman Kent's Office of National Estimates (ONE) after completing his Central Intelligence Agency (CIA) Junior Officer Training Program in June 1962. He was one of two analysts for Latin America in Kent's ONE. He was a participant in the drafting of every National Intelligence Estimate (NIE) and Special National Intelligence Estimate (SNIE) on Cuba and the Soviet military build-up from June 1962 to February 1963. This paper describes how the crisis unfolded using the author's personal recollection, declassified documents, and many memoirs written by senior CIA officers and others who were participants. Lessons learned include the need to avoid having our political, analytical and intelligence collection mind-sets prevent us from acquiring and accurately analyzing intelligence about our adversaries true plans and intentions. When our national security is at stake, we should not hesitate to undertake risky intelligence collection operations including espionage, to penetrate our adversary's deceptions. We must also understand that our adversaries may not believe the gravity of our policy warnings or allow their own agendas to be influenced by diplomatic pressure. When Soviet leader Nikita Khrushchev decided secretly to place offensive missiles in Cuba, he clearly did not believe President John Kennedy would use military action to enforce U.S. policy warnings against such a deployment.

Lacking hard intelligence to the contrary, the American Intelligence Community (IC) also issued a failed SNIE on September 19, 1962, stating Khrushchev would not place offensive missiles in Cuba. The Soviets had never before placed such missiles outside the Union of Soviet Socialist Republics (USSR) and the Warsaw Pact and the IC believed that Khrushchev certainly would not run the risk of a U.S. military response to such a provocation. Thanks to the leadership of the Director of Central Intelligence and the President, the United States overcame a political mind-set against scheduling U-2 flights directly over Cuba where they risked being shot down by Soviet surface-to-air missiles. Intelligence from an espionage agent was used by the historic U-2 flight to photograph the SS-4 medium range missiles being installed in western Cuba. An analysis of this and subsequent U-2 photography utilizing the operational manuals of the Soviet offensive missiles provided clandestinely enabled the IC to tell the President how much time he had prior to each missile site becoming operational. Soviet leader Nikita Khrushchev finally agreed to withdraw the missiles, bombers, and nuclear weapons after being convinced that the United States was preparing to launch a massive bombing and invasion of Cuba. The author concluded that such U.S. military operations were within 48-72 hours of being launched when Khrushchev publicly said the missiles would be withdrawn. There was a last minute understanding that Jupiter missiles would probably be withdrawn later from Turkey if Soviet missiles were first withdrawn from Cuba. But imminent U.S. military action was what convinced Khrushchev that the missiles had to be withdrawn.

MIND-SETS AND MISSILES: A FIRST HAND ACCOUNT OF THE CUBAN MISSILE CRISIS

INTRODUCTION – FAILED MIND-SETS

Policy and intelligence failures laid the groundwork for the 1962 Cuban Missile Crisis, the most dangerous crisis of the Cold War. This monograph will discuss and analyze the different mind-sets, or fixed mental attitudes, which policymakers and other officials brought to the task of analyzing intelligence and making foreign policy decisions. Soviet leader Nikita Khrushchev's secret policy decision to place SS-4 medium and SS-5 intermediate range missiles in Cuba was based on an erroneous assessment that once the missiles had secretly been emplaced, President John F. Kennedy would accept them as a *fait accompli*. Kennedy's perceived lack of confidence during the failed Bay of Pigs invasion of Cuba in April 1961, was one reason Khrushchev thought he could get away with placing the offensive missiles in Cuba. Khrushchev also had an ideological mind-set that believed history was on the side of socialism and communism, and that capitalism and constitutional democracy were weak and would ultimately be defeated by communism and the Soviet Union. In Khrushchev's mind-set, the extra-human forces of "history" were major drivers of political, economic, and foreign policy decisions, and he demonstrated that he was prepared to be an obedient agent of these forces, regardless of the risk of war and bloodshed. As an agent of forces that promote violent change, he nonetheless realized the utility of engaging in diplomacy as a means of possibly buying time to prepare for violent change, and even to acquire

1

allies in his efforts to have outside forces achieve their objectives.

For its part, the American Intelligence Community (IC) had a status quo mind-set that concluded Khrushchev would not place such missiles in Cuba because the Soviets had never before placed such offensive missiles outside the Union of Soviet Socialist Republics (USSR) and the Warsaw Pact. American Intelligence also thought that Khrushchev would not risk provoking the strong U.S. reaction which would certainly be generated by placing such missiles (with their nuclear warheads) in Cuba. Khrushchev, however, did not see it the way we thought he would, or the way we thought he should. Kennedy was unsuccessful in the 16-month aftermath of the failed June 1961 Vienna Summit in efforts to disabuse Khrushchev of his erroneous mind-sets about the weakness of Kennedy and the superiority of history and communist ideology.

President Kennedy activated U.S. military reserves and issued strongly worded warnings to Khrushchev emphasizing U.S. military and nuclear superiority over the USSR. But Khrushchev remained convinced that Kennedy was weak, and the United States, as a capitalist state, was doomed by history to be defeated by socialism and ultimately by communism. Only when confronted by the growing certainty of a U.S. bombing and invasion of Cuba, and the predictable obliteration of life in the Soviet Union by U.S. missiles and bombers should he choose general nuclear war, did Khrushchev step back from the precipice.

There was also a mind-set of American intelligence and policy officials that favored intelligence from technical sources, while downgrading information from human sources such as clandestine espionage agents and refugee debriefings. This mind-set was formed in part by the larger volume and greater familiarity with intelligence collected from overt technical platforms such as vehicles, ships, aircraft, and satellites. One example of this mind-set was the U.S. Air Force's use of inflated assessments of Soviet nuclear and missile strength to defend its budget. When these erroneous assessments were contradicted by intelligence from a highly valuable and reliable espionage agent, Colonel Oleg Penkovsky, a Soviet Military Intelligence officer jointly run by the Central Intelligence Agency (CIA) and British intelligence (MI-6), this information was not given the credibility it deserved until it was subsequently confirmed by our first generation Corona satellite reconnaissance.

There was also a U.S. policy mind-set that caused a delay in authorizing critical U-2 flights over the interior of Cuba. This mind-set was fearful of the political and diplomatic consequences of Soviet surface to air missiles shooting down a U-2 on the eve of the 1962 U.S. mid-term elections. This mind-set was finally overcome at the insistence of Director of Central Intelligence (DCI) John McCone who, as leader of the IC, obtained the President's approval to resume such flights in time to discover the missiles before they had become operational. Using earlier Corona photography of missiles inside the USSR and the top secret operating manuals of the SS-4 and SS-5 missiles which had been clandestinely photographed by Penkovsky and provided to the CIA and MI-6, photographic interpreters were able to identify the missiles being installed and determine when each missile site would become operational. The President thus knew how much time he had to formulate and implement a policy to convince Khrushchev to remove the missiles before having to take direct military action.

There was also a U.S. policy mind-set which sought revenge for the April 1961 defeat of the Bay of Pigs operation aimed at overthrowing Castro. The Kennedy administration mounted a second covert action to remove Castro, Operation MONGOOSE. This operation was pursued vigorously despite intelligence indicating that efforts to create an internal opposition strong enough to overthrow Castro were just not working. This mind-set even led to some consideration of assassinating Castro.

Once the missiles were discovered, it was clear to the author and others in the Office of National Estimates (ONE) that President Kennedy was unwavering in his policy commitment to remove the missiles from Cuba, either by diplomacy backed by a show of military force, or direct U.S. military action. The President announced this policy to the world in a remarkable crisis speech on October 22, 1962. All of the information and feedback the ONE staff received as a result of White House briefings attended by senior intelligence officials clearly indicated that it had been decided the missiles must be removed. Based on the evidence discussed in this monograph and the author's recollection, a U.S. bombardment and airborne invasion of Cuba were within 48 to 72 hours of being launched when Khrushchev announced publicly on October 28, 1962, that he would remove the missiles. On November 20, 1962, he also announced that he would withdraw the Soviet IL-28 bombers and the tactical nuclear weapons that had also been sent to Cuba. (Nuclear warheads for the missiles and nuclear bombs for the IL-28 bombers were also removed.)

In the end, faulty intelligence assessments and erroneous policy mind-sets were overcome when at the insistence of the DCI, U-2 reconnaissance flights resumed over the interior of Cuba. Using intelligence provided clandestinely by an on-island espionage agent, the U-2 photographed the first SS-4 missile site on October 14. (Annex C contains information on some of the Soviet and U.S. intelligence sources that were operational during the crisis; and basic definitions of clandestine operations.)

THE SEEDS OF CRISIS — 1961

The year 1961 was not a good year for the United States in the Cold War. On April 12, Soviet Cosmonaut Major Yuri Gagarin was the first person to orbit the earth in outer space. This event fueled speculation that the Soviets were ahead of the United States in the development of ballistic missiles.[1]

A counterintelligence failure came to light when British intelligence officer George Blake was arrested for espionage on April 4. He had been working for the Soviet Committee for State Security (KGB) since 1953. There was also the tragic failure at the Bay of Pigs, as CIA-trained and equipped Cuban exiles invaded Cuba in an attempt to overthrow Castro. Planning for this operation began in 1960, with President Eisenhower's concurrence, and President Kennedy approved it. Castro announced the defeat of this operation on April 20, 1961.

Other threatening events included the failure of the June 1961 summit with Khrushchev in Vienna; the building of the Berlin Wall on August 13, 1961; Khrushchev's threat to turn over access to West Berlin to the Communist East German regime; and Khrushchev's unilateral resumption of nuclear testing in the atmosphere in early September contrary to the promise he made to Kennedy at the Vienna summit.[2]

Despite all of these negative events, there was a good, albeit secret, development. Colonel Oleg Penkovsky was a Soviet army officer assigned to the *Glavnoe Razvedyvatelnoe Upravlenie* (GRU), the chief intelligence directorate of the general staff. On April 20, 1961, he arrived in London as the head of a six-man Soviet delegation from the State Committee for the Coordination of Scientific Research Work. This committee served as a cover for KGB and GRU officers who were conducting espionage to steal Western technology. However, Penkovsky had the intent of volunteering his services to the CIA and MI-6, and he was successful with the help of his host, British businessman Greville Wynne, who was cooperating with British Intelligence.[3]

The information received from Penkovsky was tightly held. There is no evidence that either Attorney General Robert Kennedy or the Assistant to the President for National Security Affairs (i.e., National Security Advisor) McGeorge Bundy knew about Penkovsky or the importance of his information. The President knew of Penkovsky, however, and took a personal interest in the "Soviet colonel's work." DCI Allen Dulles showed the President copies of Penkovsky's information, including verbatim transcripts of clandestine meetings with him. Dulles's successor, John McCone, continued to keep the President informed of the status of this case after he became DCI in November 1961.[4]

CIA and MI-6 officers met with Penkovsky for about 140 hours during his two trips to London and one to Paris. About 1,200 pages of transcripts were produced. He supplied 111 exposed rolls of film, 99 percent of which were legible. An estimated 10,000 pages or more of intelligence reports were produced from his information, which included the top secret operating manuals for the SS-4 and SS-5 missiles. The manuals had been clandestinely photographed by Penkovsky in Moscow and passed to the CIA and MI-6 in clandestine meetings in London in 1961.

By comparing the U-2 photography with information in the manuals provided by Penkovsky, analysts were able to identify positively the specific missiles being placed in Cuba and to determine on a daily basis the stage of construction of each missile site. They were, therefore, able to tell President Kennedy when each site would become operational. This information was critical in enabling the President to know how much time he had to determine and apply a policy of diplomatic and military pressure against Khrushchev before having to take direct military action.[5]

Penkovsky was one of the most important espionage agents of the Cold War. During his brief yet remarkable career, he was run jointly by the CIA and the British MI-6. Wynne served as a principal agent in contacting Penkovsky on behalf of both agencies. He arranged clandestine meetings with Penkovsky in both London and Paris in 1961 and was used to pass and receive information from Penkovsky during visits to Moscow. Brush contacts for exchanging messages with Penkovsky in Moscow were also arranged utilizing the wife of an MI-6 officer stationed in Moscow. Penkovsky came under suspicion by the KGB in about January 1962 and was never allowed to visit the West again. He also lost his access to high level Soviet military and political leaders. *Pravda* announced his arrest on December 12, 1962. The KGB would later claim that the actual date of his arrest was October 22, 1962. After a show trial in Moscow, Penkovsky's execution was announced on May 17, 1963.[6]

Soviet Deception.

In May 1961, an American journalist introduced Georgi Nikitovich Bolshakov to Attorney General Robert Kennedy. Bolshakov claimed a direct channel to Khrushchev. Bolshakov was, in fact, a Soviet GRU officer in Washington under cover as information counselor and editor of the magazine, *Soviet Life*. There is evidence of at least 51 meetings between Kennedy and Bolshakov between May 1961 and December 1962.[7]

Robert Kennedy ignored warnings from the Federal Bureau of Investigation (FBI) and the CIA that Bolshakov was a Soviet intelligence officer and thought that he had an authentic friendship with Bolshakov. He regarded Bolshakov as Khrushchev's representative but failed to realize that Bolshakov was being used to pass disinformation to the President.

Using the Bolshakov channel, the President was led to believe that Khrushchev would be willing to make concessions on nuclear testing and on Laos if Kennedy were to agree to a summit meeting. Kennedy agreed to a summit meeting in Vienna on June 3-4, 1961. Although Khrushchev and Kennedy agreed to make a cease-fire in Laos a priority, nothing else was resolved in Vienna. Khrushchev promised to end testing of nuclear weapons in the atmosphere but violated this pledge by unilaterally resuming atmospheric testing in early September 1961.

The Vienna Summit.

The Vienna Summit failed when Khrushchev threatened to sign a separate peace treaty with East Germany which would cancel all existing commitments among the four Allied powers of World War II, including occupation rights, administrative institutions, and rights of access to East and West Berlin. Khrushchev's treaty would establish the "free" city of West Berlin. There would be no interference with its internal affairs or its communications, but an agreement on access would have to be reached with the German Democratic Republic (the GDR or Communist East Germany). Western troops would be acceptable in West Berlin under certain conditions—and, of course, with Soviet troops, too. "And if there is any attempt to interfere with these plans," Khrushchev added, "there will be war." Kennedy looked straight at Khrushchev and said, "Then, Mr. Chairman, there will be war. It will be a cold winter."[8]

Kennedy met privately with James "Scotty" Reston, Washington bureau chief of the *New York Times*, in the American embassy in Vienna immediately after the summit to discuss what happened. Concerning Khrushchev's threats of war, he told Reston,

> I think he did it because of the Bay of Pigs. . . . I think he thought that anyone who was so young and inexperienced as to get into that mess could be taken, and anyone who got into it and didn't see it through had no guts. So he just beat hell out of me. So I've got a terrible problem. If he thinks I'm inexperienced and have no guts, until we remove those ideas we won't get anywhere with him. So we have to act.

Reston did not publish Kennedy's remarks until well after the missile crisis. The author also has no recollection that Kennedy's assessment of Khrushchev as expressed to Reston was ever shared with the Board or ONE. Had Kennedy's own personal assessment of Khrushchev's behavior been published or disseminated to the American IC sooner, the IC might have gotten an early sense of the dangerous mind-set which led Khrushchev to conclude that he could get away with placing offensive missiles in Cuba without triggering a U.S. military response.[9]

Former President Eisenhower tried to warn Kennedy during a conversation after the Bay of Pigs. Eisenhower asked Kennedy why he had failed to provide air cover for the landing of the CIA-trained Cuban exile force in Cuba. Kennedy responded that he had been worried the Soviets would make trouble in Berlin. Eisenhower replied, "That is exactly the opposite of what would really happen. The Soviets follow their own plans, and if they see us show any weakness, then is when they press the hardest. . . . The failure of the Bay of Pigs will embolden the Soviets to do something that they would otherwise not do." Later, Arkady Shevchenko of the Soviet Foreign Ministry reported that the Bay of Pigs "gave Khrushchev and the other leaders the impression that Kennedy was indecisive."[10]

Khrushchev's assessment of Kennedy at the Vienna Summit was shared by other Soviets. Fyodor Burlatsky, one of Khrushchev's assistants, was present at Khrushchev's debriefing after the Vienna Summit. Burlatsky thought that Kennedy seemed to Khrushchev more like "an adviser, not a political decisionmaker or president. Maybe in a crisis he would be an adviser, but not even the most influential." He thought Khrushchev looked down on Kennedy as a self-made man looks down on a rich man to whom all has been handed. At a conference in 1988, Burlatsky said that "Khrushchev thought Kennedy too young, intellectual, not prepared well for decision making in crisis situations . . . too intelligent and too weak."[11]

Khrushchev's superiority mind-set was further illustrated during a meeting on September 7, 1962, between Khrushchev and American poet Robert Frost. Construction had already secretly begun on SS-5 intermediate range ballistic missile (IRBM) sites in Guanajay, Cuba. From September 15-20, 1962, construction would begin at San Cristobal on SS-4 medium range ballistic missile (MRBM) sites. Khrushchev told Frost that the Western democracies were "too liberal to fight." President Kennedy's perceived lack of confidence during the failed Bay of Pigs invasion had convinced Khrushchev that Kennedy was "wishy-washy. . . . I know for certain that Kennedy doesn't have a strong backbone, nor, generally speaking, does he have the courage to stand up to a serious challenge."[12]

But Khrushchev's remarks to Frost reveal more than just a mind-set formed by Kennedy's handling of the Bay of Pigs, Kennedy's behavior at the Vienna Summit in June 1961, and the failure of the Western allies to react strongly to erecting the Berlin Wall on August 13, 1961. Khrushchev's assessment of Kennedy and the West was at least partially formed by communist ideology. The statement that the Western democracies are too liberal to fight is a communist tenet derived from the belief that history is on the side of socialism and communism and that the noncommunist capitalist West was weak and decadent. To a certain extent, Khrushchev was a true believer, and this mind-set influenced his assessment of events and other political leaders.[13]

Some of the people close to Kennedy had the same understanding of Khrushchev's assessment of Kennedy. Looking back in 1987, George Ball said "we all thought that Khrushchev saw him as young and weak." General Maxwell Taylor recalled that "the meeting of Khrushchev with President Kennedy in Vienna had so impressed him [Khrushchev] with the unreadiness of this young man to head a great country like the United States, plus the experience that he had seen in the Bay of Pigs [led him to believe that] he could shove this young man around any place he wanted."[14]

Following the Vienna Summit, Kennedy did, in fact, take a series of actions in an effort to disabuse Khrushchev of this assessment. But none of these actions succeeded in changing Khrushchev's personal mind-set toward Kennedy or his ideological superiority mind-set toward the United States. In a revelation of its own mind-set, the IC issued a Special National Intelligence Estimate (SNIE) on September 19, 1962, which concluded that Khrushchev would not run the risk of placing offensive missiles in Cuba because this "would be incompatible with Soviet practice to date and with Soviet policy as we presently estimate it. It would indicate a far greater willingness to increase the level of risk in U.S.-Soviet relations than the USSR has displayed thus far." But this mind-set persisted even though Khrushchev had already increased the level of risk in U.S. Soviet relations by his conduct at the June 1961 summit in Vienna; his threat to turn over the administration of Berlin to East Germany; erecting the Berlin Wall; and his testing nuclear weapons in the atmosphere contrary to his promise to Kennedy in Vienna.[15]

TECHNICAL COLLECTION VERSUS ESPIONAGE

In June 1961, an NIE concluded that the Soviets had 50-100 intercontinental ballistic missiles (ICBMs) on launchers. But Edward W. Proctor, chief of the ad hoc Guided Missile Task Force in the the CIA's Directorate of Intelligence, prepared a June 2, 1961, memorandum in which he stated that, based on the implications of a Clandestine Service report dated May 16, 1961 entitled "The Soviet ICBM Program," the previous NIE should be withdrawn and its conclusions reversed.

Proctor's memorandum was based on information Penkovsky had clandestinely provided the CIA and MI-6. Proctor argued that based on this Clandestine Service report, the Soviets had not been conducting a generally successful ICBM program, and that they did not have 50-100 operational ICBM launchers at present. They probably had 25 or fewer ICBMs on launchers. By mid-1962 they would have only 25-50 ICBMs on launchers versus the 100-200 that were projected in the June 1961 NIE.[16]

But Proctor also stated that there was a need for more information about the unknown source's credentials "because acceptance of his report as an accurate reflection of the status of the Soviet ICBM program will modify substantially our estimate and could cause important changes in U.S. policy. It is necessary that we who are assessing this program have access to almost all the information available so that we can make an independent judgment of the validity of this report." But after serious consideration by Dick Helms, CIA Chief of Operations for the Directorate of Plans; and Jack Maury, the CIA Chief of the Soviet Division in the Directorate of Plans, the decision was made against revealing further details that might point to the source of the report.[17]

No revision of the estimated number of Soviet strategic missiles was made to this June 1961 updated NIE. Although Penkovsky's information was included in the information given to the U.S. Intelligence Board (USIB) for its June 1961 update, only a brief mention was made of the report in a footnote. Members of the USIB did not argue with the Clandestine Service's evaluation of the source (Penkovsky). But a USIB member told Jack Maury that no matter how good the source was, the sub-source was unknown to consumers and was given no evaluation in the dissemination. Because of this, the sub-source "would have to be considered 'F'. The community was unwilling to accord an 'F' source any consideration in changing a National Estimate." An "F" in this case meant unsubstantiated information. The sub-source from whom Penkovsky acquired the information was Marshal Sergei Sergeyevitch Varentsov, Chief Marshal of Artillery and a mentor of Penkovsky. Varentsov was not named in the report for security reasons.[18]

A member of the USIB also recalled that "nobody wanted to accept it [Penkovsky's information] because it was so contrary to their established views and political positions, especially the Air Force. A revision would mean a change in their budget." This is a good example of how the power of government budgets can create and sustain status quo mind-sets. It also illustrates how a budgetary mind-set then worked to downgrade intelligence that contradicted and threatened the basis for the budget.[19]

Howard Stoertz, the Board of National Estimates officer in charge of estimating the Soviet strategic missile program, recalled in a 1989 interview that:

> [Though] we had a lot of technical information . . . it was incomplete. [It was] in some respects contradictory, and it was difficult to interpret. The Penkovsky information was the only piece of inside information that I can recall about Soviet thinking and planning about intercontinental missiles. His information said the Soviet Union did have a big program — like our other information indicated —

but that it was proceeding much more slowly than we had forecast. That was the critical explanation.[20]

Stoertz said that the CIA had told him that the source and his material were authentic. But he had no basis for making a judgment.

> If I had a photo taken by a U-2, I knew what it was. There was an interpreter who could tell me what was being seen. I could never talk to this source [Penkovsky] and could never find out anything about who he was. That was protecting his life, but to that extent it somewhat diminished the utility of it to me. I accepted their word, but I was looking for other confirmation.[21]

This explanation by Stoertz is an excellent illustration of the analytic mind-set that favors intelligence collected by technical means versus intelligence acquired from human espionage sources. Even if the source and sub-source had been revealed to Stoertz and other senior analysts, it is doubtful that the espionage of Penkovsky would have changed the mind-set that produced the June 1961 NIE without confirmation by U-2 or other technical collection operations.

All U-2 flights over the USSR had ceased following the shoot-down on May 1, 1960, of the U-2 flown by Francis Gary Powers. But the CIA Discoverer Satellite Reconnaissance Program, also known as Corona, had begun in 1958. After a series of failures, it began to produce photos of the USSR in August 1960. On September 6, 1961, the CIA issued a report which stated "we now believe that our present estimate of 50-100 operational ICBM launchers as of mid-1961 is probably too high." Thus Penkovsky's intelligence was correct but accepted only after confirmation by satellite photography. This again illustrates the dilemma of how properly to assess and evaluate limited, albeit likely accurate, intelligence from espionage sources, when information from other sources including technical collection is not yet available to confirm it.[22]

But it was also the information supplied by Penkovsky that enabled the photographs to be evaluated in detail and the precise capability of the SS-5 MRBMs and other missiles to be made known to the President. Without this information, the President would not have known how much time he had to negotiate before taking military action to destroy the missiles.[23]

The information that Penkovsky provided on film and in written and oral form was consistently highly evaluated up to and including the last material received from him on August 27, 1962. As of August 1963, the Penkovsky operation was described (by the CIA) as "the most productive classic clandestine operation ever conducted by the CIA or MI-6 against the Soviet target." According to authors Schecter and Deriabin, 30 years later, that judgment still holds.[24]

The purpose of espionage is to recruit foreign agents who have access to and report highly sensitive and protected intelligence, often prior to such information being available from other sources. Espionage information might be high level such as the missile manuals provided by Penkovsky or critical order of battle of information such as that provided by our espionage agent in Cuba who provided the location of an SS-4 missile site, which was then confirmed by U-2 photography. It is important, therefore, to find ways to share with senior analysts additional information about espionage sources and sub-sources to strengthen the credibility of their intelligence. Such information is now being shared extensively with analysts, particularly within centers such as the National Intelligence Council and the National Counterterrorism Center. Nevertheless, analysts must still understand that information from espionage agents with significant access may not be as abundant as intelligence from technical sources, but may well be acquired first and be just as accurate. The challenge for analysts and policymakers is to overcome previous mind-sets. They must be prepared to assess accurately and utilize espionage intelligence to preempt or mitigate crisis or disaster prior to receiving additional information from technical sources.[25]

KHRUSHCHEV PUSHES THE ENVELOPE

After the failed Vienna Summit with Khrushchev, President Kennedy gave a major speech on July 25, 1961, in which he outlined a significant increase in American nuclear forces, an increase in conventional forces in West Germany, and a call-up of military reservists in the United States. These steps had been recommended by former Secretary of State Dean Acheson at a National Security Council (NSC) meeting on June 29, 1961. They were also in line with Kennedy's recognition that he had to act to correct Khrushchev's assessment of him at the Vienna Summit. But Kennedy's hard-line speech and actions did not work. The Berlin Wall went up on August 13, 1961.[26]

The construction of the Berlin Wall was an intelligence failure. The United States and its allies were caught by surprise. Penkovsky told the CIA and MI-6 officers during a clandestine meeting in Paris in September 1961 that he had learned of plans to erect the wall 4 days before it went up; however, he had no secure way of communicating this information to us in Moscow. If President Kennedy had known of Khrushchev's intentions, he could have exposed the plan and possibly forced the Soviets to abort the mission. At the very least, the West Germans could have been alerted. Once the wall went up, the United States and its allies accepted it as a *fait accompli*. This lack of action certainly played into Khrushchev's mind-set that Western democracies were "too liberal to fight," as he was to state to Robert Frost over a year later.[27]

Khrushchev unilaterally resumed nuclear testing in the atmosphere on September 1, 1961. This violated the commitment Khrushchev made to Kennedy at the Vienna Summit that he would not be the first to resume such nuclear testing. A new NIE issued on September 21, 1961, based on Penkovsky's intelligence and photographs from the first generation Corona satellite, projected that the Soviets had fewer than 35 ICBMs. The NIE concluded that there was no missile gap. The United States had nuclear superiority over the USSR.[28]

INTELLIGENCE USED TO WARN KHRUSHCHEV

On October 17, 1961, the 22d Congress of the Communist Party of the Soviet Union opened in Moscow. On October 21, 1961, while that Congress was still in session, Deputy Secretary of Defense Roswell Gilpatric gave a speech to the Business Council at White Sulfur Springs, West Virginia. The speech was coordinated by McGeorge Bundy, Assistant to the President for National Security Affairs, and approved by President Kennedy. It called Khrushchev's bluff concerning alleged Soviet nuclear superiority. Gilpatric said, "In short, we have a second-strike capability which is at least as extensive as what the Soviets can deliver by striking first. Therefore, we are confident

18

that the Soviets will not provoke a major nuclear attack." Khrushchev did back down from his threat to Kennedy at the Vienna Summit, to sign "one way or another before this year is out," a separate peace treaty with East Germany. He said that the timing of an agreement "was no longer important."[29]

But at this same 22d Party Congress in October 1961, Soviet Defense Minister Rodian Malinovsky stated that Khrushchev's 1960 speech to the Supreme Soviet was now the basis of Soviet military doctrine. Malinovsky made it clear that because nuclear missiles were now central to Soviet doctrine, all other services had to be shaped to prepare for nuclear war. According to Khrushchev's 1960 speech, the Soviet Union was prepared to fight a nuclear war, to survive the inevitable heavy casualties, and to win. The West, on the other hand, would not survive: for them nuclear war would mean the end of capitalism. In Khrushchev's mind, the end of capitalism and the victory of socialism were inevitable.

This 1960 speech was to be the beginning of a new era for Soviet policy, which favored nuclear missiles. At the same time, Khrushchev announced a plan to reduce Soviet troops by 1.2 million men.[30]

KENNEDY LAUNCHES OPERATION MONGOOSE

At the end of November 1961, President Kennedy issued a top secret order launching what became known as Operation MONGOOSE, "to use our available assets ... to help Cuba overthrow the communist regime." The head of operations for MONGOOSE, General Edward Lansdale, reported to a new Special Group 5412 (augmented), under the direction of Attorney General

Robert Kennedy. President Kennedy constantly pushed the CIA to devise new schemes for undermining the Castro regime. MONGOOSE also included a series of plans to assassinate Castro. It was a government-wide operation involving almost all executive branch agencies. The MONGOOSE operations undertaken by the CIA were entrusted to a newly formed "Task Force W" in the CIA. Although the CIA officers assumed that the President knew of the assassination plans, there is no surviving documentary proof of this.[31]

The Special Group was initially conceived to provide authorization for every significant CIA covert action operation as specified by National Security Directive 5412/2. Under President Kennedy, members of the Special Group included the Deputy Secretary of Defense; the Under Secretary of State for Political Affairs; General Maxwell Taylor, the President's military advisor; National Security Advisor McGeorge Bundy; and the DCI. Once this group became the center of all policy and operational activity concerning Cuba, Robert Kennedy added himself to this list.[32]

In November 1961, new DCI John McCone appointed Richard Helms to be the DCI's "man for Cuba." Helms, then the acting Deputy Director for Plans (DDP), was subsequently fully appointed the DDP in February 1962. As DDP, Helms was the head of the CIA's clandestine service. Helms placed all Cuban operations in Task Force W under the command of Bill Harvey who reported directly to him. In January 1962, at a meeting in the attorney general's office, Robert Kennedy informed the senior representatives of the various agencies supporting MONGOOSE that Castro's removal from office and a change in government in Cuba were then the primary foreign policy objectives of the Kennedy administration. Repeated blunt references to "eliminating" Castro raised the question of political

assassination in peace time. According to Helms, "None of these efforts, which were first considered under the Eisenhower administration, offered anything but the slightest promise and, predictably, none went more than a step beyond the initial proposals."

Helms related that under relentless pressure from Robert Kennedy, the CIA effort under Operation MONGOOSE eventually involved some 600 CIA staff employees and between 4,000 and 5,000 contract personnel. The CIA activity ranged from establishing a refugee interrogation center to a variety of sabotage and collection operations. The steady flow of intelligence showed that Castro's military and internal security and foreign intelligence services continued to gain strength, but did not lessen the determination of the President and Robert Kennedy to even the score with Castro over the Bay of Pigs. According to Helms, "However ambitious, our sabotage efforts never amounted to more than pinpricks. The notion than an underground resistance might be created on the island remained a remote, romantic myth."

At the annual review of MONGOOSE by Robert Kennedy on October 15, 1962, he expressed the President's general dissatisfaction with the operation. The results were very discouraging. There had been no successful acts of sabotage, and one such effort had failed twice. The President had acknowledged that there had been "a noticeable improvement . . . in the collection of intelligence but that other action had failed to influence significantly the course of events in Cuba." According to Helms, the attorney general went on to point out that "despite the fact that secretaries Rusk and McNamara, DCI McCone, General Maxwell Taylor, McGeorge Bundy, and he [Robert Kennedy] personally had been charged by President Kennedy with finding a solution, only small accomplishments had been made."

The following day, October 16, 1962, the President was briefed on the U-2 photography of Sunday, October 14, which showed that the Soviets were placing MRBMs known as SS-4s at three different sites in western Cuba. MONGOOSE was temporarily overtaken by the Cuban Missile Crisis.[33]

KHRUSHCHEV DECIDES TO PUT MISSILES IN CUBA

In March 1962, Castro dismantled the Cuban Communist Party and was, at his request, given a new Soviet ambassador, Ambassador Aleksandr Ivanovich Shitov (alias Alekseev), who was the KGB chief, or resident, in Havana.[34]

Shortly thereafter, in the spring of 1962, Khrushchev decided to place offensive missiles in Cuba. Khrushchev said he made the decision during a vacation trip to Bulgaria on May 14-20, 1962. Former Chief of Staff of the Warsaw Pact Armed Forces General Anatoly Gribkov said he received orders in Moscow on May 18, 1962, to prepare a document proposing the placement of MRBMs and IRBMs in Cuba. On May 20, 1962, Khrushchev returned to Moscow, and on May 24, 1962, the Soviet Politburo and the Soviet Defense Council met and approved the proposal in principle.[35]

In May of 1962, two advisors warned Khrushchev against putting offensive missiles in Cuba. Khrushchev told First Deputy Prime Minister Anastas Mikoyan that he would secretly install missiles in September and October, but would not reveal this until after the November 1962 U.S. elections. At that time, Soviet Ambassador Dobrynin would deliver a letter to

President Kennedy announcing the existence of the missiles in Cuba. He expected Kennedy to accept the situation, as the Soviets had accepted U.S. missiles in Turkey. Mikoyan doubted the operation could be kept secret, he doubted that Castro would agree, and he doubted that the Americans would accept the missiles. Foreign Minister Andrei Gromyko told Khrushchev that "putting missiles into Cuba would cause a political explosion in the United States. I am absolutely certain of that, and this should be taken into account." Khrushchev did not heed these warnings.[36]

Thus Khrushchev decided to place offensive missiles in Cuba not only in spite of Kennedy's actions since the June 1961 Vienna summit, but also despite warnings from two senior advisors. In retrospect, it is difficult to imagine under these circumstances what the United States could have done to cause Khrushchev to change his mind. His mind-set embraced the supremacy of communist ideology, supported by the perceived weakness of Kennedy to such an extent that he even ignored the blunt advice of both his Foreign Minister and his First Deputy Prime Minister.[37]

On May 29, 1962, a high-level Soviet delegation arrived in Cuba posing as agricultural specialists to discuss the decision with Castro. The delegation included Commander of Soviet Strategic Rocket Forces Marshal Sergei S. Biryuzov. The Soviets classified strategic missiles as those with a range of over 1,000 kilometers, or about 600 miles. Mobile tactical missiles with nuclear warheads had a range of under 600 miles, and were controlled by Marshal Sergei Sergeyevitch Varentsov, Chief Marshal of Artillery. According to intelligence provided by Penkovsky, these tactical nuclear warheads were always kept in special storage depots guarded by elite KGB troops and could be distributed only after a decision by the Military Council headed by Khrushchev.[38]

At first, Castro refused to say whether he agreed with Khrushchev's offer to place the missiles in Cuba. After consulting with his inner circle the next day, Castro agreed with the plan as a gesture to improve the position of the Socialist Camp in the international arena, and not as a desperate ploy to prevent a U.S. attack. Castro did not want the Cuban people or the world to believe that Cuba could not defend itself. The Soviet delegation returned to Moscow. Final Soviet approval was given at a meeting of the Soviet Presidium on June 10, 1962. Troops for the Soviet surface-to-air missiles (SAMs) were sent to Cuba first.[39]

KHRUSHCHEV EXPLAINS HIS DECISION

Khrushchev recounted in his memoirs that he decided to place offensive missiles in Cuba for three reasons: to protect Cuba from a second "counterrevolutionary invasion" by the United States (the first was the Bay of Pigs in April 1961); to equalize "what the West calls 'the balance of power'," and to protect "Soviet prestige" in Latin America. Khrushchev worried that "if we lose Cuba . . . it would be a terrible blow to Marxism-Leninism. It would gravely diminish our stature throughout the world, but especially in Latin America."[40]

One can argue which of these three motives was the most important to Khrushchev. The author believes that the prospect of closing the missile gap with the United States by installing missiles in Cuba only 90 miles from it was the overriding strategic consideration for Khrushchev. Khrushchev discourses at length about the American missiles which "were aimed against us in Turkey and Italy, to say nothing of West Germany."[41]

Yet in a written message to President Kennedy during the crisis, Khrushchev insisted that "we had installed the missiles with the goal of defending Cuba and that we were not pursuing any other aims except to deter an invasion of Cuba." But Khrushchev also admits elsewhere, "I'm not saying we had any documentary proof that the Americans were preparing a second invasion; we didn't need documentary proof. We knew the class affiliation, the class blindness, of the United States, and that was enough to make us expect the worst." This is an excellent example of how Khrushchev's own words revealed his ideological mind-set, which even dismissed the need for intelligence and "documentary proof" about actual U.S. plans and intentions.

The only "second invasion," however, about which the author acquired any knowledge during his assignment in ONE and his work on the missile crisis, was the U.S. plan to bomb and invade Cuba to remove the missiles Khrushchev had installed there in the first place.[42] Some historians have written that "frightened by U.S. belligerency," Castro asked Khrushchev for military help, and Khrushchev responded by sending a large amount of sophisticated weaponry including offensive missiles to Cuba in the summer of 1962. The erroneous implication here is that it was Castro who was forced by "U.S. belligerency" to seek the missiles, and therefore, the United States was responsible for the Cuban Missile Crisis.[43]

But Khrushchev makes it very clear that the decision to put the missiles in Cuba was his and his alone. He states that during his vacation to Bulgaria that spring, he "had the idea of installing missiles with nuclear warheads in Cuba. . . . I knew that first we'd have to talk to Castro and explain our strategy to him in order to get the agreement of the Cuban government." In fact, Khrushchev recounts how he had arguments with Castro over this plan, but in the end Castro agreed to go along with placing missiles in Cuba.[44]

THE SOVIET PLAN

Soviet Defense Minister Rodion Malinovsky's presentation to the Presidium on June 10, 1962, made it clear that the Soviet military viewed the Cuban operation (code named ANADYR) as much an opportunity to project Soviet power into the Western Hemisphere as a rescue mission for Castro. The Presidium voted unanimously to accept the plan as put forth by Malinovsky. Under the plan, the Soviets would deploy 24 MRBMs and 16 IRBMs and would put half that many of each in reserve. The 40 missiles would be taken from units in the Ukraine and European Russia. Once installed in Cuba, they would double the number of Soviet nuclear missiles that could reach the U.S. mainland.

The Soviets would also send two cruise missile regiments which also carried nuclear warheads. They planned to send 80 of these missiles (16 launchers with five rockets each) to defend the Cuban shoreline and the region neighboring the U.S. naval base at Guantanamo. Each of these missiles had a range of about 90 miles and a nuclear charge equivalent to between 5.6 and 12 kilotons of TNT. The Soviets called these cruise missiles *"frontoviye krilatiye raketi"* or FKR.

The Soviets would also send to Cuba four motorized regiments, two tank battalions, a MiG-21 fighter wing, 42 IL-28 light bombers, 12 SA-2 units (with 144 launchers), and some antiaircraft gun batteries. Each motorized regiment had 2,500 men, and the two battalions would be outfitted with the T-55, the newest Soviet tank. The plan envisaged sending a total of 50,874 military personnel to Cuba. This structure would be an innovation for the Soviet military, which had never before included ballistic missiles in an army group.

The Soviet navy would also build a submarine base in Cuba, complete with facilities for the new Soviet ballistic missile submarine. To defend Cuba's shores, the Soviets would send two cruisers, four destroyers, and 12 Komar patrol boats each with two conventional R-15 missiles with a range of 10 miles. They would send 11 submarines, including seven that carried nuclear-tipped missiles, to patrol the East Coast of the United States.[45]

CRISIS WITHOUT OUR BEST ESPIONAGE AGENT

In July 1962, the KGB Second Chief Directorate (counterintelligence) broke out recorded conversations between Penkovsky and Wynne in a Moscow hotel room. (Penkovsky had turned on the radio and bathroom taps in an effort to defeat audio surveillance.) Wynne had been operating as a cutout and courier between Penkovsky and his CIA and MI-6 case officers. The hotel room conversation revealed that Penkovsky was an espionage agent for the West. The KGB placed Penkovsky's apartment under surveillance.

A camera was secretly placed in an adjacent apartment, and a pinhead camera was placed in the apartment above his flat. The KGB then placed poison on his chair to create a medical reason for sending Penkovsky and family away for medical recuperation. They searched his apartment and found spy gear; however, the KGB did not arrest Penkovsky. They kept him under surveillance in an effort to identify other persons who might be involved. Penkovsky also lost his access to senior Soviet military officials such as Varentsov just when the United States most needed that access and the intelligence it could have produced.[46]

SOVIET WEAPONS AND DCI WARNINGS

As it became increasingly clear that Soviet-supplied arms were flowing into Cuba, Soviet merchant shipping came under close scrutiny. Photographs of ships en route to Cuba were taken by a variety of organizations from various vantage points: from shore, from other ships, and from aircraft flying at low, intermediate, and high altitudes. The Soviets attempted to conceal and protect these shipments by covering the weapons with packing crates or by placing them in shipping containers. All of this photography was sent to the National Photographic Interpretation Center (NPIC) for analysis. The science of measuring, identifying, and cataloguing the crates and their contents became known as "cratology" and had been firmly established as an intelligence technique by the time of the Cuban Missile Crisis.[47] From July 25-31, 1962, a surge of Soviet arms shipments began to arrive in western Cuban ports. Then from August 1-5, construction began on SA-2 SAM sites in Matanzas, Havana, Mariel, Bahia Honda, Santa Lucia, San Julian, and La Coloma.[48]

Soviet military equipment and personnel were being sent to Cuba under an extensive denial and deception plan (known as Maskirovka in Russian). Soviets traveled to Cuba posing as machine operators, irrigation specialists, and agricultural specialists. Radio Moscow claimed that the Soviets were only giving Cuba "machine tools, wheat, and agricultural machinery," along with "some 7,000 tons of fertilizers." But because there was such secrecy surrounding the shipment of equipment concealed in crates and the movement at night of Soviet personnel and equipment from Cuban ports, no one in the ONE ever believed that the build-up was only agricultural. Maskirovka may have been effective in fooling persons in the Soviet government, including many of those actually involved in the shipment of the weapons. But no one whom the author knew in ONE ever doubted that a military build-up was underway.

Once we detected the installation of the SA-2 SAM sites in early August, the agricultural specialist cover of the Soviets streaming into Cuba was irretrievably blown. Moreover, the claim that the CIA paid no attention to information on the build-up that was allowed by the Cuban Government to flood Miami exile circles or that was obtained from debriefing Cuban refugees was just not true. In fact, some of the best human intelligence (HUMINT) reports we received were from exile and refugee sources. Two such reports are discussed later in this paper. But what we did not know from the beginning was just how extensive the military build-up would eventually become. The key question which ONE debated from the beginning was whether the build-up eventually would include offensive missiles that would pose a threat to our national security.[49]

On August 1, 1962, President Kennedy announced that the United States was willing to agree to a system of national control posts, subject to international supervision, for monitoring a nuclear test ban, which was a significant U.S. concession. Then 4 days later, on August 5, 1962, Khrushchev again resumed testing nuclear weapons in the atmosphere by detonating a 40-megaton explosion in the Arctic.[50]

From August 10-23, 1962, DCI McCone warned

President Kennedy a total of four times that he thought the Soviets intended to place offensive missiles in Cuba. On August 10, McCone attended a meeting with Secretary of State Rusk, Secretary of Defense McNamara, Chairman of the Joint Chiefs of Staff Taylor, Special Assistant to the President for National Security Affairs McGeorge Bundy, and others. McCone speculated that the influx of military equipment into Cuba could be used as support for the MRBMs.[51]

On that same day, McCone dictated a memo to President Kennedy expressing the belief that "installations for the launching of offensive missiles were being constructed on the island."[52] Then on August 17, 1962, McCone attended an NSC meeting that President Kennedy also attended. McCone again argued that the Soviets must be placing surface-to-surface missiles in Cuba. According to McCone, Rusk and McNamara expressed the view that the buildup was purely defensive.[53]

On August 21, 1962, DCI McCone attended another meeting with the same group that attended the August 10 meeting. He reported definite information on the installation of SAMs in Cuba. He again speculated on the probability of MRBMs being installed in Cuba. McCone gave this same information in memo form to President Kennedy the following day. On August 23, 1962, in a meeting with President Kennedy, Rusk, McNamara, General Taylor, Bundy, and others, McCone again reviewed the situation and questioned the need for the extensive SAM installations unless they were to "conceal" MRBMs.[54]

McCone's argument was based on what he called "a judgment factor." He had no hard intelligence on Soviet placement of offensive missiles in Cuba. But Penkovsky had told his American and British case officers in London in 1961 about Soviet plans to send

SAMs to Cuba and had provided a copy of the detailed manual on the capabilities of the SA-2. McCone asked himself what the SAMs were protecting because they were not protecting airfields, and he deduced that there had to be strategic offensive missiles in Cuba.

> The obvious purpose of the SAMs was to blind us so we could not see what was going on there. There they were with 16,000 men with all their ordnance equipment and then came the ships. There was nothing else to ship to Cuba but missiles. That was my argument. Other reporting was received from clandestine agents and the debriefing of refugees.

But as McCone said in a 1988 interview, "We didn't see the offensive missiles. They were on the ships, and we had no agents on the ships. We really didn't know what was on the ships, but some things you can deduce. That was one of them."[55]

McCone departed Washington on August 23, 1962, for his wedding in Seattle on August 29. He did not return to Washington until after his honeymoon in southern France on September 23.[56] However, U-2 photography on the wedding date confirmed extensive Soviet military deliveries to Cuba in recent weeks. Included were at least eight Komar-class guided missile patrol boats. These PT-like boats carry two missile launchers each, with the radar-guided missile effective against surface targets at ranges of between 15 and 17 miles. The missile carries a 2,000 pound high explosive warhead.[57]

A more detailed readout of the August 29 photography revealed the existence of another kind of missile site at Banes. It was concluded that the Banes site was a facility for launching cruise missiles against ship targets at fairly close range.[58]

31

MORE SOVIET DECEPTION

On September 1, 1962, the USSR announced publicly an agreement to supply arms and military technicians to Cuba. At a press conference, reporters asked President Kennedy for a comment on this announcement. He said that the United States would employ "whatever means may be necessary" to prevent aggression by Cuba against any part of the Western Hemisphere. The President added that "the evidence of Cuba's military buildup showed no significant offensive capability."[59]

Soviet Ambassador Anatoly Dobrynin met with Attorney General Robert Kennedy on September 4, 1962. Robert Kennedy informed Dobrynin "of President Kennedy's deep concern about what was happening" in Cuba. Dobrynin informed the attorney general that he should not be concerned. Dobrynin said he had been instructed by Khrushchev to assure President Kennedy that there would be no ground-to-ground missiles or offensive weapons placed in Cuba. Kennedy replied that it "would be of the gravest consequence if the Soviet Union placed missiles in Cuba. That would never happen, he [Dobrynin] assured me, and left." That same day, the President, after being briefed by his brother, issued a public statement that there was no evidence of "offensive ground-to-ground missiles" or of "other significant offensive capability" in Cuba. "Were it to be otherwise," he warned, "the gravest issues would arise."[60]

A readout of U-2 photography taken on the next day, September 5, revealed for the first time the presence of MiG-21 jet aircraft in Cuba. One MiG-21 was spotted at Santa Clara airfield along with crates for an additional 19 MiG-21s. The MiG-21 is a 1,000 mile per hour jet, with an altitude capability of 60,000 feet, equipped with two air-to-air infrared missiles as well as standard rockets and cannons. Cuba already had about 60 MiG-15, -17, and -19 jet aircraft.[61]

FINAL COMMUNICATION WITH PENKOVSKY

On August 27, 1962, Penkovsky exchanged packages with a CIA officer during a reception in the Moscow apartment of an American agricultural attaché. The exchange took place in a bathroom. Penkovsky's letter to the CIA described surveillance of himself and of Wynne. He alleged that Wynne had invited a Soviet boy and girl to his Moscow hotel room. He also complained that Wynne never exchanged British pounds for rubles as a normal businessman would and said that Wynne actually took rubles from him. Penkovsky then asked for a bigger resettlement bonus and promised to continue to work for the CIA and MI-6. The package he received from the CIA contained a false Soviet internal passport with his photo, but in the name of Vladimir Grigoryevich Butov. This was for Penkovsky's use should he want to make a run for it.[62]

Penkovsky subsequently appeared at an American embassy reception on September 5, 1962. There was no opportunity to exchange messages. The next day, Penkovsky appeared at the British Science and Cultural Attaché offices for a film showing. Penkovsky made eye contact with MI-6 Officer Gervase Cowell. Cowell's wife, Pamela, who was to be his new contact, was not present. There was no exchange. This was the last sighting of Penkovsky prior to his arrest.[63]

ADDITIONAL SOVIET NUCLEAR WEAPONS

Khrushchev began to secretly add to the nuclear build-up in Cuba. The Soviets had planned to put only one kind of tactical nuclear missile in Cuba, the FKR cruise missile for coastal defense. But as tension built, Soviet military leaders gave Khrushchev a list of additional battlefield nuclear weapons which could be used to counter a U.S. military invasion of Cuba. On September 7, 1962, Khrushchev authorized sending six atomic bombs for IL-28 bombers and three detachments of LUNA tactical missiles. The North Atlantic Treaty Organization (NATO) name for these tactical missiles was FROG. This missile was solid-fueled and had a range of 20-25 miles. Of the 36 LUNA missiles to be sent to Cuba, 24 had conventional warheads. Two-kiloton nuclear warheads would be sent for the other 12 missiles.

The next day, September 8, 1962, the Ministry of Defense drafted an order delegating the Soviet commander in Cuba, General Issa Pliyev, the authority to use these tactical battlefield nuclear weapons should communications with Moscow be cut and a U.S.-led invasion be underway. However, Khrushchev had already given Pliyev this authority orally during a meeting in July. Malinovsky decided not to sign or send the instructions to Pliyev in writing. According to Gribkov, even this oral authority was later withdrawn by Moscow in a cable sent to Pliyev hours before Kennedy's October 22, 1962, crisis speech, which ordered Pliyev to use "all the power of the Soviet forces" to repel an invasion, except nuclear weapons.[64]

RAPID CONSTRUCTION OF MISSILE SITES

During September the Soviets began construction of offensive missile sites. From September 1-5, 1962, construction secretly began on SS-5 IRBM sites in Guanajay. In the following 5 days, a Soviet armored group arrived at Remedios. Then from September 15-20, construction began at San Cristobal on the SS-4 MRBM sites. Construction also began at the Remedios IRBM site. Another Soviet armored group also arrived at Holguin during this same time period.

From September 20-25, 1962, construction began on SAM sites at Los Angeles, Chaparra, and Jiguani. In the next 5 days, construction began at the Sagua La Grande MRBM sites. Construction also began on SAM sites at Manati, Senado, and Manzanillo.[65]

THE DCI HONEYMOON CABLES

On September 6, 1962, McCone met with McGeorge Bundy and Roswell Gilpatric in Paris to warn them that he believed the Soviets would place offensive missiles in Cuba. In a series of cables between McCone in France and acting DCI Lieutenant General Marshall S. Carter in Washington (which became known as the honeymoon cables), McCone continued to warn about the possibility that the Soviets would place offensive missiles in Cuba.

In a cable dated September 7, 1962, McCone urged "frequent repeat missions of recent reconnaissance operations which [Deputy Secretary of Defense Roswell] Gilpatric advises informative. Also I support use of R-101 if necessary." McCone also suggested that the Board of National Estimates study the motives "behind these defensive measures which even seem to exceed those provided most satellites." Three days later, McCone cabled "difficult for me to rationalize extensive costly defenses being established in Cuba. . . . appears to me quite possible measures now being taken are for purpose of insuring secrecy of some offensive capability such as MRBMs to be installed by Soviets after present phase completed and country secured from overflights."[66]

AERIAL RECONNAISSANCE AND "THE PHOTO GAP"

Before leaving for his wedding and honeymoon, McCone said that he "left orders to overfly Cuba every day and the ship had hardly left the dock when my order was canceled by Rusk and McNamara, especially Rusk who feared a U.S. plane with a civilian pilot would be shot down and create a hell of a mess."[67]

But according to Sam Halpern, the DCI did not, in fact, have the authority to order U-2 flights. The CIA had to get approval of the Committee on Overhead Reconnaissance (COMOR) for U-2 overflights. But McCone's continued urging of overhead flights was conveyed to senior administration officials by the Deputy DCI (DDCI).

Later, in its post crisis review of intelligence, the President's Foreign Intelligence Advisory Board (PFIAB) noted that in September 1962 inclement weather delayed some of the scheduled U-2 missions. It also noted that from "September 8 to September 16, U-2 missions over Cuba were suspended apparently because of the loss of a Chinese Nationalist U-2 over the China mainland on September 8."

The PFIAB report noted that the next successful U-2 mission was not flown until September 26, 1962. No low level flights were flown over Cuba until October 23.

The PFIAB concluded that "although we were unable to establish the existence of a policy which prevented overflying areas of Cuba where surface-to-air missile installations were present, the Central Intelligence Agency and others believed that such a restriction did in fact prevail."[68]

OPPOSITION TO U-2 FLIGHTS

In his book, *Eyeball to Eyeball: The Inside Story of the Cuban Missile Crisis*, Dino Brugioni clearly describes the continued opposition of Rusk and Bundy to any overflights in the wake of the shoot down of the Chinese Nationalist U-2 over China. One can understand how the CIA and others thought there was a policy against such flights over Cuba when proposals for such overflights were continually opposed by these two senior-level foreign policy officials.

In the wake of this shoot down, a Special Group meeting was scheduled on September 10 in the Bundy's office to discuss aerial reconnaissance over Cuba. At that meeting, both Rusk and Bundy questioned the need to overfly Cuba. Rusk was concerned that a U-2 being shot down over Cuba would generate a crisis similar to the Francis Gary Powers shoot down over the Soviet Union in May 1960. Rusk, supported by Bundy, said that the Kennedy administration faced a number of problems concerning the continued use of the U-2. The United Nations (UN) had convened in September, and congressional elections were coming up in November 1962. The downing of a U-2 could have dramatic repercussions. Couldn't intelligence objectives be met by peripheral reconnaissance flights using oblique photography? The reconnaissance experts at this meeting tried to point out to Rusk that slant photography to avoid SAMs would produce poor results.[69]

It is important to note that Brugioni was one of the original 12 who, under the direction of Arthur C. Lundahl, organized the NPIC. During the missile crisis, Brugioni was the chief of a unit responsible for providing all-source collateral information to photo interpreters. Every morning, Lundahl would review the all-source intelligence before taking it to the USIB and the Executive Committee (EXCOM) of the NSC. Returning from these briefings, Lundahl would inform his staff chiefs, who included Brugioni, of the recipients' reactions and their continuing intelligence needs. Lundahl was an astute observer, and Brugioni made detailed notes of what Lundahl had seen and heard so that the NPIC might better respond to the concerns and needs of policymakers. The CIA photo-exploitation shop was founded in the early 1950s and had invited other organizations to join. Two days before President Eisenhower left office in January 1961, it was renamed the NPIC. This NPIC continued as a joint CIA-military organization until the late 1990s.[70]

Brugioni noted that during the September 10 meeting, Attorney General Robert Kennedy became impatient with Rusk, stating at one point, "Let's sustain the overflights and the hell with the international issues." Robert Kennedy supported a CIA proposal, which had McCone's strong support, to conduct a single high level U-2 flight to cover the Banes cruise missile area as well as the areas not covered during the August 29 and September 5 missions. Rusk was still concerned about so much time over Cuban territory. He thought the mission would be too exposed. Finally, Kennedy looked at Rusk and said, "What's the matter, Dean, you chicken?"[71]

The next day, Rusk, still fearful of a U-2 loss, even asked the State Department Legal Officer to investigate the possibility of having U-2 flights conducted under the auspices of the Organization of American States (OAS). He made a similar request to the Department of Defense (DoD). Given the need to provide at least 6 months training to OAS pilots, it was doubtful that U-2 overflights would ever be resumed if pilots had to be non-Americans. The DoD General Counsel then responded to Rusk on September 12 that the transfer of U-2 flights would not be legally permissible either under the UN or OAS charters.[72]

A compromise was reached. Four short flights would be substituted for one long overflight. It was not clear what sort of missions these were to be. On September 17, a U-2 peripheral mission was authorized by the President. By the time the U-2 reached the Cuban coast, the weather forced the abortion of the mission. Under the new rules for peripheral flights, all reconnaissance aircraft were to fly no closer than 25 miles from the Cuban shore, the slant range of the SA-2 SAMs. Peripheral flights by aircraft other than the U-2 produced photography that was not usable. The first successful U-2 peripheral flight was flown on September 26, 1962. Its targets were areas that had been covered before. The second successful peripheral U-2 mission was flown on September 29 and covered the Isle of Pines and the Bay of Pigs area. A new SA-2 and a cruise missile site were discovered. Two other peripheral U-2 flights were flown on October 5 and 7, 1962. Their photography revealed more SA-2 SAM sites, but no offensive strategic missiles.[73]

THE FAILED ESTIMATE

On September 13, 1962, President Kennedy again issued a public warning to the Soviets against placing offensive missiles in Cuba.[74] After issuing two warnings to the Soviets on September 4 and 13, President Kennedy called for a SNIE. On September 19, this SNIE was approved by the USIB and sent to the President. It concluded the following:

> [T]he USSR could derive considerable military advantage from the establishment of Soviet medium and intermediate range ballistic missiles in Cuba, or from the establishment of a submarine base there. As between the two, the establishment of a submarine base would be the more likely. Either development, however, would be incompatible with Soviet practice to date and with Soviet policy as we presently estimate it. It would indicate a far greater willingness to increase the level of risk in US-Soviet relations than the USSR has displayed thus far, and consequently would have important policy implications with respect to other areas and other problems in East-West relations.[75]

Just prior to forwarding this estimate to the USIB for final approval and dissemination to the President, Sherman Kent called a meeting of his entire staff and all members of the Board of National Estimates. At this meeting, Kent summarized the situation as follows: The DCI thinks the Soviets are placing offensive missiles in Cuba. He doesn't have any information we don't have, but he is convinced that the Soviets will or are doing so. The estimate at hand says that we think they aren't and that they won't. (The estimate had already been worked over by the rest of the American IC, including the U.S. military.) There is no hard evidence that they will. Most importantly there was no overhead photography proving that they are.

Kent asked everyone in the room to express his or her opinion on this subject. He went around the room calling everyone by name. No one was left out, not even the junior Cuban analyst.[76] Kent wanted to know who supported the DCI's view, who did not, and why. The author supported the view of one of the Board Members who thought that the Soviets were certainly willing and able to place offensive missiles in Cuba, but would take a "salami slice" approach before doing so. According to this view, the Soviets would first place a submarine base in Cuba. Then, depending on the U.S. reaction, they would move to place offensive missiles in Cuba. The author recalls that no one at the meeting took or supported the DCI's position. The consensus was that there was not enough convincing information or evidence to support the DCI's view. As Sherman Kent put it with characteristic exasperation and flair, "We can't just tell the President that we think the Soviets will put missiles in Cuba because Khrushchev is a son-of-a-bitch. The President knows he's a son of a bitch." He added that as an intelligence organization, we are supposed to have the necessary evidence. And we didn't.[77]

With the stakes so high, great emphasis was placed on aerial reconnaissance. A few recent reports from human sources had indicated that offensive missiles were being placed in Cuba, but the reports were not enough in quantity or detail to overcome doubts which arose in the absence of photographic proof. In retrospect, the author wonders how many staff and Board Members were unaware, as was he, that there had been no successful U-2 flights over or even around the periphery of Cuba from September 5 until September 26. The author does not recall this fact being mentioned at all during that critical all-hands meeting of the staff and Board Members just prior to the release of the estimate on September 19. Brugioni had personally informed Kent that there had been no U-2 coverage of Cuba's interior since the September 5 mission. But Kent immediately interrupted and said "that's another ball game that we are not to get involved in." He was probably thinking about Rusk and Bundy's continuing opposition to overhead coverage of the interior.[78]

SHERMAN KENT REFLECTS

In an essay entitled "A Crucial Estimate Relived" written in 1964 and declassified and published in 1994 by the Center for the Study of Intelligence, Kent recounts the lack of human source reporting that had been received by the time the SNIE was published on September 19, 1961. This is true. Several excellent reports were acquired during the first week of September, but not received by clandestine means or acquired by debriefings until after September 19. Kent also pointed out that "nor did the aerial photography of September dissipate the uncertainty. Not only did it fail to spot the ominous indicators of missile emplacement, but over and over again it made fools of ground observers by proving their reports inaccurate or wrong."[79]

But there were no U-2 flights over western and central Cuba from September 5 until early October. There were no flights of any kind, even peripheral, from September 5 until September 26. There was, therefore, no way aerial photography could have played a role in proving or disproving human source reporting during that critical time prior the SNIE being disseminated on September 19. It would appear that notwithstanding Brugioni's briefing, Kent simply did not know the full extent of the lack of reconnaissance flights. The author recalls that among the ONE staff, there was the assumption, even mind-set, that the lack of reconnaissance intelligence meant that the U-2 had flown but not found any missile sites. But the lesson is that a lack of intelligence is not intelligence. It is just that—a lack of information.[80]

Kent had reviewed the five reports which in hindsight indicated that the Soviets might be placing offensive missiles in Cuba. Sidney Graybeal, the CIA offensive missile expert, reviewed these same reports and concluded that there were errors in them. Graybeal affirmed that all of the reported information and sites had been checked against aerial photography. Kent was satisfied and reviewed the estimate for a final time. But there simply was no aerial photography against which these reports could be checked. There were no flights over the interior of Cuba from September 5 until October 14—a total of 39 days.

The peripheral flight scheduled for September 17 was cancelled due to bad weather. The peripheral flights that were made on September 26 and 29 and October 5 and 7 revealed more SAM sites but no offensive missiles. There were, therefore, no flights of any kind, peripheral or over the interior, from September 5 until September 26—7 days after the estimate was released. It would appear that Graybeal, like Kent, may not have fully understood this absence of reconnaissance photography.[81]

In addition to an understandable overemphasis on technical collection, there was also an overreliance on the credibility and effectiveness of U.S. policy in convincing Khrushchev not to place offensive missiles in Cuba. Those of us in ONE knew how determined the President and his administration were to prevent the Soviets from placing offensive missiles in Cuba.

We got a feel for the heat of that policy determination from senior CIA officials who dealt with the White House and from the strength of the President's public warnings. Underlying our deliberations, therefore, was our own mind-set that surely Khrushchev must have understood the strength of the President's policy resolve the way we did. He did not. There were miscalculations on both sides. By September 19, however, it is doubtful that Khrushchev could have convinced the Presidium that it was necessary to reverse the gears of Operation ANADYR based solely on President Kennedy's public warnings.[82]

According to John T. Hughes, Special Assistant to DIA Director Lieutenant General Joseph F. Carroll during the missile crisis, strategic warning is the most important element of effective intelligence. But perhaps the greatest barrier to developing strategic warning for policymakers is "the tendency of the human mind to assume that the status quo will continue." Hughes said that several crises and conflicts after World War II, including the Cuban Missile Crisis, confirm that "nations do not credit their potential opponents with the will to take unexpected acts. We did not believe the Soviets would do so in 1962."[83]

MCCONE FORCES APPROVAL OF OVERFLIGHTS

When McCone returned to Washington from his honeymoon in late September, he asked for a map showing the actual U-2 coverage of Cuba since the September 5 mission. That map showed that outside of coastal areas, very little information about Cuba's interior had been obtained. According to Lundahl who was present at that meeting, "McCone nearly came out of his chair when he saw the map." McCone then called for a special meeting of the Special Group for October 3, at which he took Secretaries Rusk and McNamara to task. He was very concerned with statements being made by spokesmen from the Departments of State and Defense to the effect that there were no offensive missiles in Cuba. McCone pointed out that there had been no aerial reconnaissance over central or western Cuba for over a month, and that all flights since September 5 had been of limited penetration or peripheral. McCone said that as the President's leader of the American IC, he could make no definitive statement that there were no offensive missiles in Cuba. He then said he would so inform the President.[84]

Rusk still objected to the overflights because a U-2 shot down over Cuba would be difficult for the administration to explain. Bundy also still insisted that the United States should try to achieve its reconnaissance objectives by flying peripheral missions. McCone then provided information clearly showing that peripheral missions could not confirm or deny the presence of offensive missiles. McCone said he would seek permission for a number of short flights over Cuba to cover the entire island based on targets with intelligence priorities. These plans would be presented to the Special Group on October 9.[85]

At this meeting, the COMOR Committee agreed to conduct U-2 overflights from south to north. The highest priority was the western portion of the island, especially over the trapezoidal area reported in secret writing by an espionage agent as being located near San Cristobal in Pinar Del Rio Province. This area was heavily guarded by Soviets where "very secret and important work is in progress, believed to be concerned with missiles." That same day the Special Group approved the COMOR recommendation for four U-2 south-to-north overflights that would cover most of Cuba. The group also recommended transferring reconnaissance responsibilities for Cuba to the Strategic Air Command (SAC). The SA-2 sites were by then mostly operational, and further overflights had to be considered dangerous. McCone agreed. The President approved the four overflights, and the stage was finally set for the fateful October 14 U-2 mission #3101. This was the flight over western Cuba that first discovered Soviet SS-4 MRBMs being installed.[86]

The insistence of the DCI on overflights as opposed to continued peripheral flights was a critical factor in obtaining the President's approval for the October 14 flight. McCone was correct in his assessment that the SA-2 sites had been established "to blind our reconnaissance eye." But ironically the SA-2 had been effective in a way that possibly even McCone had not anticipated. Their discovery combined with the fear caused by the shoot-down of the Chinese Nationalist U-2, led Rusk and Bundy to undertake self-induced blindness by opposing flights over the interior. It was blindness achieved without firing a shot. McCone deserves the major credit for pushing the administration out of what was a politically "safe" mind-set of peripheral flights and into overdue U-2 coverage of the interior of Cuba. (The lesson here is that potential risks and dangers to national security often require dangerous and high-risk intelligence collection operations. A policy mind-set that avoids such intelligence collection when the stakes are as high as they were in Cuba can produce even greater threats to our national security.)[87]

THE DECEPTION CONTINUES

On October 6, 1962, Bolshakov told Robert Kennedy that he had met with Khrushchev and Mikoyan during a vacation on the Black Sea in mid-September 1962, and that Khrushchev told Bolshakov to assure President Kennedy that "no missile capable of reaching the United States will be placed in Cuba." Mikoyan added that only SAMs were being installed in Cuba.

The following day, American journalist Charles Bartlett invited Bolshakov to lunch to ask for his message in writing on behalf of President Kennedy. This message was repeated and passed to Kennedy again. Theodore Sorensen later recalled that "President Kennedy had come to rely on the Bolshakov channel for direct private information from Khrushchev, and he felt personally deceived. He was personally deceived."[88]

INTELLIGENCE NOT DISSEMINATED

On October 11, 1962, McCone showed President Kennedy photographs of crates loaded on the deck of a ship which arrived in Havana in early October. These crates were presumably carrying IL-28 Soviet medium range bombers. President Kennedy requested that such information be withheld until after the U.S. elections. McCone replied that this was not possible. This information had been disseminated to the IC and several military commands. President Kennedy then asked that the report state the probability that the crates contained the bombers because no bomber had yet been seen. McCone agreed.

The President then asked that all future information be suppressed to which McCone replied that this would be dangerous. It was agreed that such information would be disseminated to members of the USIB with instructions that only those responsible for giving the President advice be given the information. A minimum number of experts within the CIA would also be informed.[89]

In its post-crisis report, the PFIAB stated that the DCI instructed the CIA analysts in May 1962 to check any report with NPIC that was susceptible to photographic verification. Although the purpose of this instruction was to establish by all available means the authenticity of refugee and agent reports, it was interpreted by the CIA analysts as a restriction against publishing anything, including espionage and refugee debriefing information, that could not be verified by the NPIC from aerial reconnaissance. Although this analytical mind-set was formed by an incorrect interpretation of the DCI's instructions, it did result in delaying the dissemination of human source information pending the receipt of U-2 photography.

The President also contributed to the delay in disseminating intelligence concerning possible Soviet missiles by instituting the tightest possible control of all information concerning offensive weapons in Cuba. He wanted such information collected, analyzed, and reported to officials with a real need to know. The USIB interpreted this Presidential instruction as an injunction against printing any information on offensive weapons in Cuba in any intelligence publication.[90]

MISSILES DISCOVERED

On Sunday, October 14, 1962, a U-2 took the first photos of a SS-4 MRBM site at San Cristobal, Cuba. The U-2 photos, plus copies of the top secret Soviet manuals for the SS-4 and SS-5 missiles clandestinely photographed by Penkovsky during 1961 in Moscow, would enable the Guided Missile and Astronautics Intelligence Committee (GMAIC) and the Joint Atomic Energy Intelligence Committee (JAEIC) to determine the stage of construction of each missile site on a daily basis. The IC could tell Kennedy when each site would become operational.[91]

The author remembers receiving and disseminating within ONE, three very specific reports that have since been declassified and which led to the fateful U-2 flight on October 14. One was a report from an espionage agent in Cuba who reported a conversation with the personal pilot of Fidel Castro. The pilot confided on September 9, 1962, that "we have 40-mile range guided missiles, both surface-to-surface and surface-to-air, and we have a radar system which covers, sector by sector, all of the Cuban air space and (beyond) as far as Florida. There are also many mobile ramps for intermediate range rockets. They don't know what is awaiting them." But this report was not disseminated to the IC until September 20, the day after the Special National Intelligence Estimate was disseminated. This delay was most likely due to the time required for the agent to securely transmit the information to the CIA case officers.[92]

The author recalls quickly passing this report to the ONE staff and board. The source was directly quoting Castro's pilot, who would have been in a position to have acquired the information from traveling with and being in the presence of Castro, and overhearing privileged conversations. It was this access to Castro, and the source's directly quoting the pilot, that gave this intelligence report particular significance. This report was enough to convince the author that the Soviets were placing offensive missiles in Cuba.

Another report contained information from a refugee debriefing. The refugee saw 20 trucks with long trailers driven by Soviets during the night of September 12, 1962, in the Mariano district of Havana. The refugee described a long object under wood and canvas extending beyond the end of the trailers. The source described the fins of the object and even drew a picture of the missile silhouette and tail fin silhouette. Then using photographs, he identified the object as a Soviet SS-4 SHYSTER MRBM missile. But this report was not disseminated until September 27, eight days after the SNIE was disseminated. The author distinctly recalls that this report was highly convincing, particularly since the refugee drew an accurate picture of the SS-4 missile, including its tail fin! He then identified the missile from photographs. This was an excellent detailed debriefing that contained information which appeared to be accurate.[93]

Another important agent report was distributed on September 18, 1962, the day before the SNIE was disseminated. It reported that as of September 7, there was a large restricted military zone in Pinar del Rio Province. The report provided the coordinates of the four cities that bounded this restricted area. These cities were San Cristobal, San Diego de los Banos, Consolacion del Norte, and Las Pozas. The report also described strict security to prevent access to the finca (farm) of a Dr. Corina, where "very secret and important work is in progress, believed to be concerned with missiles." The coordinates were also given for the location of this finca. A refugee also separately reported seeing a convoy of Soviet flat-bed trailers carrying large tubes extending over the end of the trailers, heading toward Pinar del Rio province on September 17. This report was distributed on October 1.[94]

The above agent report, which contained the coordinates in Pinar del Rio Province, was never adequately credited for helping find the missiles. On September 15, the agent conveyed the information in secret writing in a letter mailed from Cuba via international mail to an accommodation address in a foreign city. It was the trapezoid formed by these four cities that became the photographic target of the U-2 flight on October 14 that first photographed the Soviet SS-4 missiles. Prior to that date, the area of Cuba described by the agent had not been photographed by a U-2 flight since August 29. As previously mentioned, operational control of the U-2 flights over Cuba was officially transferred from the CIA to the Joint Chiefs of Staff/SAC on October 12, 1962. On October 13, the CIA U-2 detachment at Edwards Air Force Base was transferred to McCoy Air Force Base in Orlando, Florida, which would become the U-2 operating base.[95]

Former DCI Richard Helms, in his memoir, *A Look Over My Shoulder,*" stated that it was the agent report concerning the large restricted zone in Pinar del Rio province that convinced the White House to request a U-2 flight over the San Cristobal area. It was 4 days before the weather cooperated, but just before midnight on October 13, a U-2 piloted by U.S. Air Force Major Richard S. Heyser took off from Edwards Air Force base in California and headed for San Cristobal, Cuba. This flight first photographed the construction of MRBM sites near San Cristobal. Major Heyser landed at McCoy Air Base in Orlando, Florida. He described it as a "milk run," but it might also be counted as one of the most significant reconnaissance missions in history.[96]

The film of this mission (an entire roll was 5,000 feet long) was then rushed to waiting aircraft for transfer to the Naval Photographic Intelligence Center in Suitland, Maryland. The photo-analysts identified an SS-4 MRBM launching site, and two SS-5 intermediate range missile sites under construction. The latter weapons had a range of over 2,000 miles and could reach many major U.S. cities, much of eastern Canada and northern South America. After the crisis, Ray Cline asked both Robert Kennedy and McGeorge Bundy if they would assess "how much that single evaluated piece of photographic evidence [the San Cristobal SS-4 sites] was worth. . . . [T]hey each said it fully justified all that the CIA had cost the country in all its preceding years."[97]

Much has been written about the above Cuban agent report. One author, Max Holland, refers to the report as coming from "a Cuban observer agent, the lowest rank in the intelligence pecking order, who had been recruited under MONGOOSE." But in the world of espionage, the value of an agent's information is determined by his or her access to priority intelligence and the agent's history of reporting reliability, not necessarily the agent's rank in a government hierarchy. If the priority collection requirement is order of battle information, as it was in Cuba during the Soviet military build-up, then a reliable observer on the ground who has visual access to important military activity can be just as important as overhead photography or a senior espionage agent inside the Cuban or Soviet Government. This "observer agent" was actually even more important than our Soviet espionage agent Penkovsky, who by then had come under suspicion by the Soviets and had lost his access.[98]

The above human source reports, two from espionage agents and one from a refugee, were not received in time to have any effect on the SNIE of September 19. But after that date, intelligence analysts and especially the ONE should have considered what to do with this new information which seemed to contradict the finding of the SNIE. In retrospect, it would seem that perhaps ONE should have issued a brief statement summarizing this new information and the reliability of the three sources, thus alerting the White House and the IC to the possibility that the estimate was wrong. We did not issue such a statement.

If anything, the tendency in ONE generally was to react to new human source intelligence by simply waiting and assuming that U-2 aerial reconnaissance would follow-up and prove or disprove it. But unknown to the author, and presumably other ONE and the CIA analysts, domestic political concerns of the administration would prevent meaningful overflight coverage of Cuba until the DCI returned from his honeymoon and insisted that such coverage be reinstated. This would, therefore, turn out to be an example of a political mind-set which prevented overhead U-2 reconnaissance, while a separate mind-set simultaneously required such technical intelligence before believing and disseminating important human source intelligence. The perennial challenge for intelligence analysts and policymakers will remain how to analyze and evaluate correctly espionage and other human source intelligence in the absence of technical confirmation. (In an era characterized by the proliferation of weapons of mass destruction [WMD], particularly nuclear weapons, our national security, and indeed our very survival, may well depend on whether we learn how better to handle this challenge in the future.)[99]

Crisis Management.

On the evening of Monday, October 15, 1962, Bundy was briefed on the discovery of the missiles by Ray Cline, the CIA Deputy Director of Intelligence. Bundy decided not to brief the President until the following morning. He thought that a hastily-called meeting that same evening could give away the secret of the missile discovery. In any event, nothing could be done until the following morning. He thought that the best course for the President was for him to get a good night's sleep after a strenuous campaign weekend.[100]

On Tuesday morning, October 16, 1962, President Kennedy was briefed on the discovery. The President established an EXCOM of the NSC, by NSC Memorandum 195 (which he actually signed on October 22, 1962). The EXCOM met secretly beginning on October 16 to advise him on how to respond to the crisis.[101]

The following were members of the EXCOM: Attorney General Robert Kennedy, Secretary of State Dean Rusk, Secretary of Defense Robert McNamara, Secretary of the Treasury Douglas Dillon, National Security Advisor McGeorge Bundy, Chairman of the Joint Chiefs of Staff Maxwell Taylor, President's Special Counsel Theodore Sorensen, Under Secretary of State George Ball, DCI John McCone, and Soviet specialist from the State Department Llewellyn Thompson. In addition, former Secretary of State Dean Acheson, John McCloy, Robert Lovett, and others were consulted. The President tape recorded the meetings without the participants' knowledge, and transcripts are now available.[102]

Others who participated in the EXCOM either as experts or in place of their superiors were Latin

America Assistant Secretary of State Edwin M. Martin, Deputy Undersecretary of State for Political Affairs U. Alexis Johnson, Deputy Secretary of Defense Roswell Gilpatric, Assistant Secretary of Defense for International Security Affairs Paul H. Nitze, Deputy Director of the CIA General Marshall Carter, Kenneth O'Donnell, Adlai Stevenson, and U.S. Information Agency Deputy Director Donald Wilson. Dean Rusk recommended that Dean Acheson become a member of the EXCOM because of his quick grasp of complex issues. The President approved.[103]

Although a member of the EXCOM, Vice President Johnson was not present for EXCOM meetings during the first week of the crisis. He returned to Washington from a campaign trip to Hawaii on October 21 and was briefed that day by McCone and Lundahl on the discovery of the missiles.[104]

According to General Taylor, after being briefed at the October 16 White House meeting on the discovery of the missiles in Cuba, President Kennedy "gave no evidence of shock or trepidation resulting from the threat to the nation implicit in the discovery of the missile sites but rather a deep but controlled anger at the duplicity of the Soviet officials who had tried to deceive him." According to Lundahl, the President said he wanted the whole island covered, he didn't care how many missions it took. "I want the photography interpreted and the findings from the readouts as soon as possible."[105]

At a follow-up meeting in Secretary McNamara's office, McNamara was told that the maximum number of U-2 missions that could be flown daily with existing assets would be six, flying from early morning to late in the evening. It was decided that both SAC and the CIA U-2 pilots would cover all of Cuba. The CIA pilots would be used only in "extreme circumstances," and they would be recommissioned into the Air Force and given Air Force credentials. The U.S. Navy's Light Photographic Squadron No. 62 was selected to conduct low-altitude reconnaissance over Cuba. Hurricane Ella delayed additional flights over Cuba until October 17 when a total of six U-2 missions were flown, along with a massive electronic intelligence (ELINT) collection effort on the part of the military services and the National Security Agency (NSA).[106]

On the morning of Wednesday, October 17, the staff of ONE was informed about the missile discovery. The impact was one of shock and anger. We had all been worried and concerned about this possibility given the espionage and refugee source reporting that had been received. The lid was clamped down tight on any further dissemination of this knowledge to anyone outside of ONE. The EXCOM met three times during the day to discuss what action the United States should take. Different views and alternatives were discussed but in the end, there was a firm agreement that the missiles had to be removed from Cuba. The author recalls no retreat from that unshakable policy commitment throughout the crisis.[107]

Also on October 17, DCI McCone went to Gettysburg to brief former President Eisenhower and to get his views on what to do. Eisenhower leaned toward military action which would cut off Havana and therefore take over the heart of the government. He thought this might be done by airborne divisions, but was not familiar with the size of the Cuban forces in the immediate area or their equipment.[108]

SOVIET DECEPTION AND PRESIDENTIAL WARNING

Soviet Foreign Minister Gromyko made a previously planned visit to the White House on Thursday, October 18, accompanied by Soviet Ambassador Dobrynin. Gromyko assured President Kennedy that offensive missiles would not be placed in Cuba. President Kennedy repeated his public warning and again pointed out the serious consequences that would arise if the Soviet Union placed missiles or offensive weapons in Cuba. Gromyko assured him this would never be done, and that the United States should not be concerned. Kennedy displayed a remarkable calm during the TV and photo coverage of that White House visit, as he listened to the Soviets lie to him 2 days after he received the U-2 photos of the MRBM site in western Cuba.[109]

ESTIMATES LEAD TO POLICY DECISIONS

The President departed Washington on Friday, October 19, for campaign appearances in Chicago. That same day, a SNIE was written to evaluate the probable Soviet reactions to certain U.S. courses of action in Cuba. The SNIE concluded that "a major Soviet objective of the Soviet military buildup in Cuba was to demonstrate that the world balance of forces has shifted so far in their favor that the U.S. can no longer prevent the advance of Soviet offensive power even into its own hemisphere." It also concluded that,

> if the U.S. takes direct military action against Cuba, the Soviet Union would not attack the U.S., either from Soviet bases or with its missiles in Cuba, even if the latter were operational and not put out of action before

they could be readied for firing. Since the USSR would not dare to resort to general war and could not hope to prevail locally, the Soviets would almost certainly consider retaliatory actions outside Cuba. . . . We believe that whatever course of retaliation the USSR elected, the Soviet leaders would not deliberately initiate general war or take military measures, which in their calculation, would run the gravest risk of general war.[110]

Also on October 19, a joint evaluation of the Soviet missile threat was prepared by GMAIC, JAEIC, and the NPIC. This evaluation of the MRBM (NATO designation SS-4) and the IRBM (NATO designation SS-5) missile sites drew heavily on Penkovsky's information. Based on U-2 photography and this documentary information from Penkovsky, one of the SS-4 regiments which has a total of eight launchers and 16 missiles was considered operational. Two SS-5 sites with a total of eight launchers were under construction near Havana. One site would be operational in six weeks, and the other could be operational between December 15-30, 1962.

Although the evaluation stated that one nuclear warhead storage facility was under construction near the SS-5 sites, it also stated "there is no evidence of currently operational nuclear storage facilities in Cuba. Nevertheless, one must assume that nuclear weapons could now be in Cuba to support the operational missile capability as it becomes available." The evaluation also said that "There are several refugee reports indicating the presence of tactical [FROG] missiles in Cuba, although there is no photographic confirmation thus far." As noted earlier, FROG is the NATO designation for the Soviet LUNA Tactical Missile. It is interesting to note that only after U-2 photography confirmed the presence of offensive missiles in Cuba, was reporting on the Soviet military build-up from human sources such as espionage agents and refugees given serious credibility.[111]

Another SNIE was written on Saturday, October 20, to assess the major consequences of certain U.S. courses of action with respect to Cuba. The estimate stated that any naval blockade of Cuba would not place the Soviets under immediate pressure to choose a military response. Should the United States use force against Cuba, the likelihood of a Soviet response by force, either locally or elsewhere, would be greater than in the case of blockade. This estimate repeated the conclusion that the Soviets would not attack the United States in response to military action against Cuba, even if the Soviet missiles in Cuba were operational and not put out of action. While acknowledging the possibility that the Soviets might miscalculate, the estimate repeated that the USSR would almost certainly not resort to general war, but would consider retaliation outside of Cuba. The estimate added that "a rapid occupation of Cuba would be more likely to make the Soviets pause in opening new theaters of conflict than limited action or action which drags out."

The estimate concluded that there were four MRBM and two IRBM sites under various stages of construction. The MRBM had a range of about 1,100 nm and the IRBM a range of about 2,200 nm. Sixteen launchers for MRBMs must be considered operational now. In addition, the inventory of other weapons then included 22 IL-28 jet light bombers, one of which was assembled and three others which were uncrated.

According to this estimate, the inventory also included 39 MiG-21 jet fighters, of which 35 were assembled and four still in crates; and 62 other jet fighters of less advanced types. There were 24 SA-2 sites, of which 16 were believed to be individually operational with some missiles on launchers. There were three cruise missile sites for coastal defense, of which two were operational. The estimate also reported 12 Komar cruise missile patrol boats; all were probably operational or nearly so.[112]

The IL-28 had a combat radius of about 750 miles. There was considerable discussion within the staff and the Board of National Estimates as to whether the IL-28 should be considered an offensive weapon. These bombers could strike parts of the southeastern United States and were eventually included with the missiles as offensive weapons which were removed from Cuba. It is interesting that Secretary McNamara expressed his opinion at an EXCOM meeting on October 17 that if nuclear warheads were supplied to the MRBMs, then the Soviets would also supply nuclear bombs for bombers with offensive capability.[113]

THE PRESIDENT DECIDES TO BLOCKADE

After a telephone call from Robert Kennedy, the President returned to Washington that Saturday from a campaign trip to the mid-west feigning a cold. The afternoon meeting began with an intelligence briefing by McCone and Ray Cline, the Deputy Director of Intelligence. Cline covered the points made in the October 20 SNIE discussed previously. Secretary McNamara specifically referred to this estimate and its conclusion that the Soviets would not use force to push their ships through a blockade. After additional discussion, the President decided to implement a naval blockade or quarantine as a first step. Air strikes and invasion could follow if the quarantine was not successful in forcing the Soviets to remove the missiles. The President decided to delay the quarantine to permit consultation with our allies.[114]

During this critical meeting, General Taylor and National Security Advisor Bundy wanted to start with an air strike while everyone else wanted to start with a blockade. Robert Kennedy argued that a surprise attack could not be undertaken if the Unites States were to maintain its moral position at home and around the globe.

During the meeting, lines were clearly drawn between the groups that would later be labeled "doves" and "hawks." Doves included McNamara, Stevenson, Rusk, and apparently Sorensen, who were against following up the blockade with an air strike. They preferred negotiations with the Soviets over U.S. missiles in Turkey, Italy, and the U.S. base in Guantanamo, Cuba. The President sharply rejected the thought of surrendering Guantanamo in the present situation. Rusk wanted to delay a decision on the next step until after a blockade, which he preferred to call a "quarantine." Joining Taylor and Bundy as hawks were Robert Kennedy, Dillon, and McCone who wanted the blockade to serve as an ultimatum to be followed by an air strike.

This meeting was not tape recorded because it was held in the Oval Room on the second floor of the Executive Mansion and not in the West Wing of the White House. Based on the notes of participants, however, President Kennedy approved the blockade as well as actions necessary to put the United States in a position to undertake an air strike on the missiles and missile sites by Monday or Tuesday. He also said that he was prepared to authorize the military to take those preparatory actions which they would have to take in anticipation of the military invasion of Cuba. The President stated flatly that the Soviet bombers in Cuba did not concern him particularly. He said we must be prepared to live with the Soviet threat as represented by these bombers. They did not affect the balance of power, but the missiles already in Cuba were an entirely different matter.

When General Taylor returned to the Pentagon after the meeting, he told the Joint Chiefs of Staff: "This was not one of our better days." He added that the President had said, "I know you and your colleagues are unhappy with the decision, but I trust that you will support me in this decision." Taylor said he had assured the President they would. General Earle G. Wheeler, Chief of Staff of the Army, remarked: "I never thought I'd live to see the day when I would want to go to war."[115]

MILITARY STRIKE REVIEWED

At a meeting on Sunday, October 21, with President Kennedy, Attorney General Robert Kennedy, Secretary McNamara, General Taylor, and DCI McCone, the plans were reviewed in considerable detail for an air strike against the missile bases, the air fields, and a few SAM sites in critical locations, as well as for an invasion. General Taylor was instructed to plan for the necessary air strike. There was complete agreement that military action must include an invasion and occupation of Cuba.

Secretary McNamara and General Taylor told the President that an air strike could not provide absolute assurance that all missiles would be destroyed. They indicated a 90 percent probability. They also stated that any warning would probably cause missiles to be moved to unknown locations. General Taylor therefore recommended that the air strike be conducted immediately, suggesting the next morning, and without warning. Secretary McNamara confirmed the above military appraisal but made no recommendation as to policy.

In response to direct questioning from the President, the attorney general and DCI McCone advised against a surprise attack "for the reasons discussed at previous meetings." The attorney general did not make an absolute recommendation about future military action, indicating action could be decided as the situation developed. Only preparatory steps should be taken now. McCone urged the President to indicate publicly the intention to remove the missiles and other weapons by "means and at a time of his own choosing," if surveillance proved that the Soviets and Cubans were not removing them.[116]

BRIEFING IKE, LBJ, AND ALLIES

On Sunday, October 21, 1962, the DCI briefed Eisenhower a second time, at McCone's residence. Lundahl accompanied the DCI to explain the photography. Eisenhower went along with the "suggested plan of initiating a blockade, conducting intense surveillance, and announcing the intention of taking military action if the Soviets and the Cubans either maintained the status quo of their missile installations or continued the construction of their missile bases. The military actions he [Eisenhower] envisaged would be air strikes and invasion."[117]

Also on that Sunday, at the request of the President, McGeorge Bundy, the DCI, and Lundahl briefed Vice President Johnson. Johnson "favored an unannounced strike rather than the agreed plan which involved blockade and strike and invasion later if conditions warranted." However, the Vice President agreed reluctantly to a blockade after learning of Eisenhower's support.[118]

Also on Sunday, teams traveled abroad to brief our allies: Prime Minister John Diefenbaker in Canada, Prime Minister Harold MacMillan in Britain, and West German Chancellor Konrad Adenauer. All were supportive. French President Charles de Gaulle was briefed at mid-day on Monday, October 22, by Acheson and Kent. Kent recalled that de Gaulle asked, "Are you here to consult with or to inform me?" "I am here to inform you," replied Acheson. Despite this rather cool beginning, Kent felt "delighted at the great interest de Gaulle showed in these photographs. When told that the photographs had been taken from a height of 14 miles, de Gaulle exclaimed 'C'est formidable! C'est formidable!'" The general asked if Kennedy had considered the possibility that the Russians might move in Berlin. Acheson replied that it had been considered, but should the Russians move, it would mean war. De Gaulle assured Acheson that it would not come to war. He then assured Acheson that Kennedy could count on his support. "It's exactly what I would have done," he added.[119]

Upon his return, Kent briefed the staff and the Board of the ONE. At a packed meeting, Kent said that he and Acheson had been prepared for a difficult meeting with the French President. Kent recounted de Gaulle's question about being consulted or informed and that de Gaulle was told quite frankly by Acheson that he was being informed. But overall Kent said he was pleasantly surprised at how well the briefing of de Gaulle had gone. According to Kent, de Gaulle was both satisfied and supportive of the intelligence briefing and of President Kennedy's decision.[120]

On Monday October 22, 1962, the President briefed leaders from Congress, and the American Embassy in Moscow delivered a copy of Kennedy's speech to Khrushchev 1 hour before the President went on national television.[121]

THE PRESIDENT'S ADDRESS AND DEFCON 3

President Kennedy made a television address to the nation that Monday evening, October 22, 1962. This was one of the best and most powerful crisis speeches of the 20th century.

> But this secret, swift, and extraordinary build-up of communist missiles — in an area well known to have a special and historical relationship to the United States and the nations of the western hemisphere, in violation of Soviet assurances, and in defiance of American and hemispheric policy — this sudden, clandestine decision to station strategic weapons for the first time outside of Soviet soil — is a deliberately provocative and unjustified change in the status quo which cannot be accepted by this country if our courage and our commitments are ever to be trusted again by either friend or foe.[122]

The staff in ONE were relieved that the awful secret they had been carrying around and guarding for the previous 6 days was finally public knowledge. There had been no leaks. We could now acknowledge and discuss the crisis with other Agency officers. We could acknowledge to spouses and families that the crisis explained at least in part our recent grim countenances and late working hours, although long tense days were not all that unusual in ONE. After the President's speech had ended, we knew that we had successfully kept the secret. We were now ready as a government and as a people to unite in confronting this nuclear threat to the security and the existence of our nation and potentially to all other nations of the free world.[123]

On that same day, the Pentagon placed the entire U.S. military establishment on Defense Condition (DEFCON) 3, an increased state of alert. This was the greatest mobilization since World War II. SAC B-47 bombers were dispersed to over 30 civilian airfields in the United States. At SAC bases in Spain, Morocco, and England, B-47 bombers were loaded with nuclear weapons. A massive airborne alert was begun by U.S.-based B-52 bombers which were loaded with nuclear weapons and by KC-135 tankers. Most communications between headquarters and the B-52 bombers were in the clear. The Soviets would intercept these communications and would thus fully understand the scope and seriousness of the growing U.S. military response.[124]

The alert lasted for 30 days of continuous flight operations—2,088 sorties in 48,532 continuous hours of flying time, in which 20,022,000 miles were flown without a fatality. Over 70 million gallons of fuel were transferred in flight by the KC-135 tankers.[125]

Just as the Germans thought that General George Patton was the best commander the Allies had in World War II (and Patton agreed), so General Curtis Lemay was perhaps the American leader most feared by the Soviets during the Cuban Missile Crisis. General Lemay was Chief of Staff of the U.S. Air Force, whose command responsibilities included the bombers of the Strategic Air Command. He was perhaps the ultimate "cold warrior," and the Soviets knew it. In one of his talks to SAC crews, he was quoted as saying, "There are only two things in this world, SAC bases and SAC targets." Khrushchev knew that the SAC had targeted specific Soviet cities for immediate destruction in the event of war and that "city busting" was being advocated by General Lemay to bring the USSR quickly to its knees. This Soviet fear of General Lemay, coupled with their ability to listen to SAC communications which were deliberately not enciphered, may well have been an important factor in Khrushchev's ultimate decision to back down and withdraw offensive weapons from Cuba. General Lemay may well have been one of the most important and most under-rated players in the missile crisis.[126]

Secretary McNamara received word in the evening of October 22 that 91 Atlas and 41 Titan liquid-fueled ICBMs were being readied for firing. The solid-fuel Minuteman ICBM would enter the inventory during the late days of the crisis. Polaris submarines took up positions in the North Atlantic with enough nuclear missiles to destroy all of Russia's principal cities. Matador and MACE tactical cruise missiles in West Germany were brought to combat-alert status.[127]

Also on October 22, the Pentagon asked the Association of American Railroads for 375 flatcars immediately to move air-defense and air-warning units to Florida. Later, the Pentagon would ask for 3,600 flatcars, 180 gondola cars, 40 boxcars, and 200 passenger coaches to move the over 15,000 men and equipment of the 1st Armored Division from Texas to Georgia. Some elements of the division would move to southern Florida where they would bivouac at the Gulf Stream Park Race Course at Hallandale, Florida. Parking lots became motor pools. Some soldiers slept in the grandstands; others picnicked or played touch football in the infield. Although no racing program was going on at Gulf Stream, troops enjoyed lining up along the rails to watch the thoroughbreds work out during the early morning hours.[128]

The presence and activities of the troops from the 1st Armored Division at the race course were clearly visible to the population in the area and to motorists on the adjacent public highways and roads. This public build-up of ground forces was one more method of getting the message to the Soviets that the United States was preparing not only to bomb, but also to invade Cuba. This would add further credibility to the stated U.S. policy of not allowing offensive missiles to be established in Cuba.[129]

DEFCON 2

President Kennedy signed the order for the naval quarantine on Tuesday, October 23, 1962. That same day, Secretary of State Rusk obtained a unanimous concurrence from the OAS to support the naval quarantine of Cuba.[130]

Also on October 23, Soviet Defense Minister Malinovsky, following an emergency meeting with Khrushchev and the Soviet Council of Ministers, placed the Soviet armed forces on a war footing. Marshal Andrei Grechko, Commander of the Warsaw Treaty Forces, increased the combat readiness of these forces. But there were no threatening moves by the Soviet army in Berlin or by the Soviet naval forces in the Mediterranean. According to Sam Halpern, the Soviets never called up their reserves, there were no conscript classes called up, and there was no assembling of aircraft, trains, or ships. In short, there was no Soviet mobilization.[131] Later on that Tuesday evening, NSA flashed word to the CIA watch office that its direction-finding efforts indicated that Soviet ships bound for Cuba that were suspected of carrying missiles, had not only changed course, but were probably on their way back to Russia.[132]

The next day, Wednesday, October 24, the Joint Chiefs of Staff issued DEFCON 2, a maximum alert with the optimum posture to strike either Cuba or the USSR or both. With DEFCON 2, a total of 1,436 bombers and 134 ICBMs were on constant alert. The missiles were ready for launching and one-eighth of the bombers were in the air at all times. The rest of the air crews were waiting near their bombers, ready to take off at a moment's notice. That evening, a Pentagon spokesman confirmed that "at least a dozen Soviet vessels have turned back, presumably because, to the best of our information, they might have been carrying offensive materials." Other vessels still proceeded toward Cuba.[133]

Late that Wednesday evening, President Kennedy called Secretary McNamara to confirm when our forces would be ready to invade Cuba. McNamara replied, "In 7 days." When the President pressed whether all the forces would be well prepared, McNamara replied that they would be "ready in every respect in 7 days."[134]

Initial Reaction.

On Wednesday, October 24, Bartlett showed the U-2 photos of missiles in Cuba to Bolshakov over lunch at the National Press Club. Bolshakov denied any knowledge of offensive missiles in Cuba.[135] That same day, the official world reaction showed a generally favorable response to the U.S. action, particularly in Latin America. On Tuesday, October 23, the OAS representatives had approved a resolution endorsing the naval quarantine without opposition. One abstention was due to a lack of home government instructions. There were no indications of any Soviet aircraft movement to Cuba. Measures to achieve a higher degree of action readiness for Soviet and Bloc forces were not being taken on a crash basis. But existing MRBM and IRBM sites in Cuba were being rapidly completed, as were buildings believed to provide storage for nuclear warheads.[136]

Aerial photography of Cuba on October 24 and 25 clearly showed that work on the missile sites was moving ahead rapidly, even faster than before. The nuclear warhead storage building at San Cristobal site No. 1 had been completely assembled in 2 days. Two IL-28 Beagle bombers had been assembled, three more were in the process, and crates for an additional 20 bombers were at San Julian airfield.[137]

DCI McCone reported that as of 6 o'clock Thursday morning, October 25, at least 14 of the 22 Soviet ships that were known to be en route to Cuba had turned back. Those that turned back had a history of carrying military cargo.[138] On that same day, U.S. Ambassador to the UN, Adlai Stevenson, displayed the U-2 photos to the UN Security Council, winning a major public relations victory for the United States. Soviet Ambassador Valerian Zorin replied only that, "We shall not look at your photographs."[139]

Official Soviet Reaction.

At 7 o'clock on Friday morning, October 26, the first vessel was stopped and boarded under the quarantine. It was the *Marucla*, an American-built liberty ship, Panamanian-owned, registered from Lebanon, and bound for Cuba under a Soviet charter from the Baltic port of Riga. The vessel was found to contain no weapons and was allowed to sail on. The *Marucla* was carefully and personally chosen by President Kennedy to be the first ship stopped and boarded. It demonstrated that the United States was indeed going to enforce the quarantine. But because the ship was not Soviet-owned, this action did not represent a direct threat to the Soviets requiring a response. This gave the Soviets more time, but simultaneously demonstrated that the United States meant business.[140]

That same day, Aleksandr Semyonovich Feklisov (alias "Fomin"), the KGB resident in Washington, replaced Bolshakov as the conduit between Khrushchev and Kennedy. He asked for a meeting with John Scali of the American Broadcasting Company (ABC) and asked if the United States would accept a deal whereby the USSR withdraws all offensive missiles under UN supervision and the United States agrees not to invade Cuba. This would, in fact, be the primary basis for an eventual agreement.[141] Also on October 26, Khrushchev sent a long emotional message to Kennedy with the same offer as was conveyed by Feklisov to Scali. The following day, Saturday, October 27, a Soviet SA-2 missile shot down a U-2 aircraft over Cuba, killing the pilot, U.S. Air Force Major Rudolf Anderson, Jr. The U-2 was shot down using Moscow's order dated October 22 authorizing Pliyev to use all defensive means against the United States, except for nuclear weapons. Pliyev's deputy had authorized the downing of the U-2 by SAMs.[142]

Khrushchev sent a second message on Saturday, October 27, broadcast publicly on radio, adding the condition that the United States withdraw Jupiter missiles from Turkey. Based on the suggestion of his brother Robert, and supported by Sorensen, the President decided to ignore the second message and accept the first. Robert Kennedy and Sorensen then drafted the reply. It stated that if the Soviet missiles and offensive weapons were removed from Cuba

71

under UN inspection and verification, the United States would agree with the rest of the Western Hemisphere not to invade Cuba.[143]

THE DARKEST DAY

Saturday, October 27, 1962, was the darkest day of the crisis. The Soviets continued the rapid construction of missile sites and had shot down and killed U-2 pilot Major Anderson. The State Department analyst assigned to ONE for Latin America informed the author that the two of them had been assigned the responsibility of drafting a new SNIE. The subject was the probable reaction of governments in Central and South America to U.S. air strikes followed by an invasion of Cuba. The OAS had previously unanimously approved a U.S. naval blockade of Cuba, but a bombardment and invasion of Cuba was a different matter.

The earlier August 1, 1962, NIE on the situation and prospects in Cuba stated that there was widespread disillusionment in Latin America regarding the Cuban Revolution. We did not think that any Latin American government (other than Cuba) was truly comfortable with the presence of Soviet strategic nuclear missiles in the Western Hemisphere particularly because these same missiles could reach much of Latin America, as well as the United States. We thought that most Latin American governments were relieved that President Kennedy in his October 22 speech had placed the entire hemisphere under the protective umbrella of U.S. conventional and strategic forces. We, therefore, concluded in our draft that should diplomacy and the naval quarantine fail to force the Soviets to remove their offensive missiles from Cuba, most Latin American governments would support a U.S. bombardment and invasion of Cuba. A few would probably criticize such military action publicly, but would most likely support it privately.[144]

That we had been asked on such short notice to draft this SNIE was another strong indicator that the United States was indeed preparing to bomb and invade Cuba. U-2 coverage continued to show accelerated construction of the missiles sites in Cuba. Some were becoming operational. This, plus the shoot-down of Major Anderson, led the two of us to speculate that military action would probably begin on or about Tuesday, October 30. This speculation was based on recent events and the policy firmness of the White House that the missiles must be withdrawn. The author was not aware of the October 24 conversation between President Kennedy and Secretary McNamara in which McNamara twice assured the President that the U.S. military would be ready "in every respect" to bomb and invade Cuba in 7 days, i.e., on October 31. This draft SNIE was never finished. The next day, Sunday, October 28, Khrushchev announced publicly that he would withdraw the missiles from Cuba.[145]

On Saturday, five of the six MRBM sites were believed to have a full operational capability. The sixth was estimated to become operational on Sunday, which meant that the Soviets would then have the ability to coordinate the launching of up to 24 MRBM missiles within 6 to 8 hours of a decision to do so. There would be a refire capability of up to 24 additional missiles within 4 to 6 hours. At that point, 33 MRBM missiles had actually been observed. No IRBM missiles had yet been observed. The probable nuclear bunkers adjacent to the MRBM sites were not yet ready for storage, assembly, or checkout. Aerial photography from October 25 confirmed the presence of a FROG missile launcher in a vehicle park near Remedios.[146]

THE FINAL WARNING

On Saturday evening, October 27, Robert Kennedy met with Soviet Ambassador to the United States Anatoly Dobrynin in Kennedy's Justice Department office. He delivered the President's reply to Khrushchev's message from the previous day. Kennedy told Dobrynin that the President must have a commitment by the following day, October 28, that the offensive missile bases would be removed. "I was not giving them an ultimatum but a statement of fact. He [Dobrynin] should understand that if they did not remove those bases, we would remove them."

Dobrynin raised the question of the Jupiter missiles in Turkey. Kennedy said there could be no quid pro quo under the current threat and that ultimately this was a decision which would have to be made by NATO. However, President Kennedy had wanted to remove those missiles for some time, and it was his judgment that they would be removed within a short time after the current crisis was over. That same evening, the President ordered 24 troop-carrier squadrons of the Air Force Reserve to active duty. They would be necessary to support an invasion.[147]

On Sunday, October 28, the CIA published a memorandum, "The Crisis, USSR/Cuba," prepared for the EXCOM. "All 24 MRBM launchers now appear to have reached full operational readiness. One nuclear storage facility is essentially complete, but none of the bunkers observed is yet believed to be in operation."

No significant redeployment of major Soviet ground, air, or naval forces had been noted. The general posture of Soviet ground forces in forward areas was one of precautionary defensive readiness.

Khrushchev's attempt to get reciprocal withdrawal of offensive weapons from Cuba and Turkey appeared to be the first step in Soviet efforts to negotiate a solution. Soviet spokesmen continued to play down the possibility that the Cuban crisis could lead to general war. There was so far only fragmentary mixed reaction to the President's rejection of Khrushchev's Cuba-Turkey proposal.[148]

Khrushchev publicly agreed on Sunday, October 28, to remove the missiles in return for a U.S. pledge not to invade Cuba. There was an implicit promise to remove Jupiter missiles from Turkey later.[149]

AFTERMATH

The Special Group (5412 Augmented) called a halt to the sabotage component of Operation MONGOOSE on October 30. This Special Group was abolished. Covert action against Cuba, however, did not end. At the end of 1962, the EXCOM was renamed the Standing Group and reduced in size to five members: McNamara, McCone, Bundy, Sorensen, and Robert Kennedy.[150]

On November 2, 1962, two voiceless telephone calls were made in Moscow to a telephone number given by the CIA to Penkovsky for his use to indicate that he had loaded a dead drop. The telephone pole had the signal of a letter X in chalk indicating the drop had been loaded. Richard Jacob, the U.S. Embassy archivist, was sent to unload the drop. He was ambushed and arrested by the KGB. The man in charge of his arrest was Lieutenant General Oleg Gribanov, head of the KGB Second Chief Directorate (responsible for internal security and counterintelligence). Gribanov had also supervised the earlier search and arrest of Penkovsky. Jacob was declared persona non grata and departed the Soviet Union on November 6.[151] Wynne was also arrested in Budapest on November 2. The following day, DCI McCone briefed President Kennedy on the ambush of Jacob and Penkovsky's probable arrest.[152]

On November 20, 1962, the Soviets decided on their own to withdraw the IL-28 bombers, their six nuclear bombs, and the tactical nuclear weapons. Castro was unhappy: He had hoped to keep the tactical weapons in Cuba.[153]

The CIA published a memorandum on November 29 concerning the deployment and withdrawal of Soviet missiles and other weapons in Cuba. The Soviet claim that they had actually delivered only 42 missiles to Cuba and had now withdrawn them was consistent with the CIA evidence. Available evidence also indicated that the Soviets were preparing to withdraw the IL-28 bombers, no more than 42 of which were delivered before the quarantine began. The Soviets could easily ship out all of these aircraft by mid-December 1962.

Other Soviet weapons systems in Cuba included SAMs, coastal defense missiles, Komar missile boats, and fighter aircraft. In addition, the equipment for four armored combat groups (including possibly 6-10,000 men) remained on the island. The CIA had no evidence of any preparations in Cuba to withdraw these elements.[154]

Nuclear warheads were not actually seen in Cuba until the post-crisis review of aerial photography taken during the crisis period. Photo coverage from October 14 revealed a nuclear warhead processing facility at the western end of the runway at the Mariel Naval Airfield. On October 23, one of the warhead vans at the San Cristobal MRBM launch site had its rails extended and appeared to be transferring a warhead to a truck that had parallel rails in its beds. The post-crisis review of photography also indicated that the Soviets had fueled and mated the warheads and had practiced moving the missiles to the erectors.

At a January 1989 conference of American and Soviet leaders in Moscow, Soviet General Dmitri Volkogonov said that during the crisis 20 nuclear warheads arrived in Cuba and 20 more were aboard the Soviet merchant ship *Poltava*, which turned back when the blockade was announced. Sergei N. Khrushchev, son of Nikita Khrushchev, said that the 20 nuclear warheads in Cuba were never mated to the missiles but easily could have been.[155]

MISSILES IN CAVES

There was a surge of intelligence reporting after the crisis, mostly from refugees, that the Soviets had secreted some of the offensive missiles in caves. None of these reports was judged to be accurate. On February 5, 1963, DCI McCone issued a formal unclassified statement in the name of the USIB. In it, he said, "We are convinced beyond reasonable doubt, as has been stated by the Department of Defense, that all offensive missiles and bombers known to be in Cuba were withdrawn soon thereafter. . . . [R]econnaissance has not detected the presence of offensive missiles or bombers in Cuba since that time." Concerning the alleged storage of missiles in caves, McCone said, "All statements alleging the presence of offensive weapons are meticulously checked. So far, the findings have been negative. Absolute assurance on these matters, however, could only come from continuing penetrating on-site inspections." Such inspections, however, were never agreed to or permitted by Castro.[156]

On February 6, 1963, Secretary McNamara introduced an unclassified briefing in the State

Department auditorium. He said, "In recent days questions have been raised in the press and elsewhere regarding the presence of offensive weapons systems in Cuba. I believe beyond any reasonable doubt that all such weapons systems have been removed from the island and none have been reintroduced. It is our purpose to show you this afternoon the evidence on which we base that conclusion." After this introduction, John Hughes, the Special Assistant to the Director of DIA, presented a detailed photographic review of the introduction of Soviet military personnel and equipment into Cuba, and of the removal of offensive weapons systems.[157]

THE PRESIDENT'S FOREIGN INTELLIGENCE ADVISORY BOARD

In its February 4, 1963, memorandum to the President, the PFIAB stated:

> In the course of our review, we sought to determine whether there were lessons to be learned from an objective appraisal of the strengths and weaknesses of the U.S. foreign intelligence effort as disclosed by the Cuba experience. We directed particular attention to those areas of the intelligence process which are concerned with such matters as (1) the acquisition of intelligence, (2) the analysis of intelligence, and (3) the production and dissemination of intelligence reports and estimates in support of national policy formulation and operational requirements.

The Board reviewed the performance of our intelligence prior to the October 14, 1962, discovery of offensive missiles. There was inadequate clandestine agent coverage within Cuba, and full use was not made of aerial photographic surveillance, particularly during September and October. Pointing to the failed NIE from September 19, 1962, the Board concluded that there was a malfunction of the analytic process by which intelligence indicators are assessed and reported. The manner in which intelligence indicators were handled may well have been the most serious flaw in our intelligence system which, if not corrected, "could lead to the gravest consequences."

> Concerning espionage, the PFIAB concluded the following: Clandestine agent coverage within Cuba was inadequate. Although the limited agent assets of the CIA and Army intelligence did produce some valuable reports on developments in Cuba, we believe that the absence of more effective clandestine agent coverage, as an essential adjunct to other intelligence collection operations, contributed substantially to the inability of our government to recognize at an earlier date the danger of the Soviet move in Cuba. It would appear that over the years there has been a lack of foresight in the long-term planning for the installation of these agents.

The PFIAB also concluded that:

> full use was not made of aerial photographic surveillance, particularly during September and October when the influx of Soviet military personnel and armaments had reached major proportions. We recognize that in September inclement weather delayed some of the scheduled U-2 missions. However, we note that from September 8 to September 16, U-2 missions over Cuba were suspended apparently because of the loss of a Chinese nationalist U-2 over the China mainland on September 8. We also note with concern that during the period of increasing emergency, as pointed up by intelligence indicators, there was not a corresponding intensification of the scheduling of U-2 missions over the island.

The Board concluded that although they were "unable to establish the existence of a policy which prevented overflying areas of Cuba where surface-to-air missile installations were present, the Central Intelligence Agency and others believed that such a restriction did in fact prevail." As we now know, "full use was not made of aerial photographic surveillance" due to the opposition of Rusk and Bundy to flights over the interior of the island. This opposition was based on their concern about the political and diplomatic repercussions if a U-2 had been shot down over Cuba. The lack of "intensification of the scheduling of U-2 missions over the island" was due to this opposition and not to a failure of the DCI or the CIA to seek such intensification. In fact, we have seen how the DCI consistently warned about the Soviets placing offensive missiles in Cuba and continually pushed for increased U-2 coverage over Cuba. The PFIAB report, however, fails to note this and leaves the reader with the impression that somehow the CIA and the American IC were responsible for this "lack of intensification."

Apparently the Special Group responsible for authorizing U-2 flights was also not made fully aware of the delay in the acquisition of aerial intelligence and neither was most of the American IC. Delays were not only due to weather, but also to the decision of senior administration officials to fly only peripheral flights. The Special Group should have been informed of the delay in overflights and should have had a mechanism to discover automatically such reporting omissions.[158]

On March 7, Bundy sent a copy of the PFIAB report and the DCI's February 28, 1963, memo response to the President to President Kennedy's secretary for filing. He noted that, "These are explosive documents, and their existence is not being widely discussed." It is not clear what Bundy meant by "explosive documents," but he was certainly aware that it was his and Secretary Rusk's opposition that prevented U-2 flights over Cuba, rather than a failure of the IC or the DCI. There is one PFIAB document dated March 11, which indicated McCone thought that unless the report was changed, the top five people in the CIA, including the DCI, would have to resign. We have no indication the report was changed, and there were no resignations.[159]

But McCone's February 28 memo has been declassified. It is remarkably low key and non-inflammatory. In his February 28, 1963, memorandum to the President, McCone said that while he agreed with some of the PFIAB's findings, he thought that his own study of the crisis reflected a "more reasonable judgment" of the IC's performance. Concerning the failure to exercise urgency in con-ducting U-2 missions over Cuba, he demonstrated sympathy and understanding for Rusk and Bundy's actions by stating one "must first carefully weigh the serious considerations that enter into a decision to overfly a denied territory." Concerning the failed September 19, 1962, SNIE, he noted that everyone got it wrong, "including the State Department." Concerning espionage agent reports, none that had significant information on offensive missiles reached the IC or policymakers until after mid-September. "When received they were used in directing aerial photograpy."

The Board also criticized the failed September 19 SNIE as due to:

A lack of adequate intelligence coverage of Cuba; the rigor with which the view was held that the Soviet Union would not assume the risks entailed in establishing nuclear striking forces on Cuban soil; and the absence of an imaginative appraisal of the intelligence indicators which, although limited in number, were contained in reports disseminated by our intelligence agencies. (We reach this conclusion even though we recognize the absence at the time of any conclusive photographic intelligence.)[160]

The PFIAB concluded:

> We believe that the near-total intelligence surprise experienced by the United States with respect to the introduction and deployment of Soviet strategic missiles in Cuba resulted in large part from a malfunction of the analytic process by which intelligence indicators are assessed and reported. This malfunction diminished the effectiveness of policy advisers, national intelligence estimators, and civilian and military officers having command responsibilities. [161]

The Board attached 35 examples of such indicators as an annex to its report. "We urge that the annexed illustrations be read not only for their individual content but also for the purpose of noting the cumulative significance of the information being received. These indicators were acquired from a variety of individual sources, such as refugees, clandestine agents, and friendly foreign diplomats." As previously noted, the Board concluded that the way these intelligence indicators were handled may well be the most serious flaw in our intelligence system, which, if not corrected, "could lead to the gravest consequences."[162]

As was previously noted, the Board discovered that the CIA analysts had interpreted the DCI's instruction to check with NPIC on any report susceptible to photographic verification as a restriction against publishing anything that could not be verified by NPIC. The President also imposed another limitation as discussed before. He made it clear that he wanted no limitation on the collection and analysis of intelligence relating to offensive weapons and all such information was to be collected, analyzed, and promptly reported to those officials who had a real need to know. He wanted the tightest possible control of all information concerning offensive weapons. The USIB, however, interpreted the presidential instructions as an injunction not to print any information on offensive weapons in Cuba in any intelligence publication. After this injunction, even the President's Intelligence Checklist prepared by the CIA failed to include information from any of the refugee or agent reports on the sightings of offensive missiles in Cuba.[163]

The Board noted, however, that the photographic evidence from the October 14 and subsequent overflights was promptly processed and submitted to the President in time for decisive action before the Soviet MRBM and IRBM systems became fully operational. In commending the high performance achieved by "our foreign intelligence agencies during the post-October 14 period, we recognize that it would be difficult for the IC to operate with the same intensity and efficiency under less critical conditions. Thus one of our major problems remains the achievement of very high performance between crises."[164]

In commenting on lessons learned from the crisis, Robert Kennedy wrote:

> The time that was available to the President and his advisers to work secretly, quietly, privately, developing a course of action and recommendations for the President, was essential. If our deliberations had been publicized, if we had had to make a decision in 24 hours, I believe the course that we ultimately would have taken would have been quite different and filled with far greater risks.[165]

McNamara has written:

> The performance of the U.S. Government during that critical period [of the Cuban missile crisis] was more effective than at any other time during my 7 years' service as Secretary of Defense. The agencies of the government: the State Department, the civilian and military leaders of the Defense Department, the CIA, the White House staff, the UN Mission, worked together smoothly and harmoniously. [166]

While McNamara gives Robert Kennedy much of the credit for this performance, the President made no statement attempting to take credit for himself or for the administration. He instructed all members of the EXCOM and government that, "no interview should be given, no statement made, which would claim any kind of victory. . . . [I]f it was a triumph, it was a triumph for the next generation and not for any particular government or people."[167]

As previously mentioned, after the crisis the CIA's Deputy Director of Intelligence Cline asked Robert Kennedy and Bundy how much they thought the single evaluated U-2 photograph of the MRBM site on October 14, 1962, was worth. They both replied, "It had fully justified all that the CIA had cost the country in its preceding years." But without espionage and DCI leadership, there would have been no photograph. The prior cost of the CIA would not have been justified. This U-2 photograph was the result of intelligence from an espionage agent who described probable MRBM sites in a trapezoidal area of western Cuba. This combined with the unwavering insistence by the DCI as the President's leader of American Intelligence that reconnaissance flights over the interior of Cuba be resumed, led President Kennedy to reverse the previous opposition to such flights within his own administration.

For a brief yet momentous time in our history, DCI and Presidential leadership successfully combined to produce accurate intelligence. Our national security system worked and possible disaster was avoided. It may not be possible in future crises to ensure the same high quality of national security leadership. For its part, however, the American IC can and must always strive to improve the collection and analysis of all source intelligence, particularly intelligence from espionage. This will alway be one of the keys to successful national security leadership.[168]

KHRUSHCHEV RESIGNS

On October 13, 1964, 2 years after the missile crisis, Khrushchev resigned all of his party and government offices. By 1964, Khrushchev had alienated a majority of the Presidium. Although the main source of discontent had been his continual reorganization of the party and the state apparatus, the Cuban missile crisis played a role in his downfall. It was resented as a Soviet humiliation, not as a victory as Khrushchev had earlier proclaimed.[169]

LESSONS LEARNED

A number of lessons can be learned from the collection, analysis, and use of intelligence in the Cuban Missile Crisis which have broad and continuing applicability. First, we must realize the danger of allowing a predetermined mind-set to blind intelligence analysts and policymakers to evidence of the probable or ongoing actions of an adversary. Khrushchev's conviction that the West, in general, and the young U.S. President, in particular, were weak and indecisive led him to discount how far the U.S. leadership would go to stop a new and dangerous threat to its security. This mind-set was further bolstered by Khrushchev's ideological conviction that Communism was destined to defeat capitalism. Conversely, the mind-set of U.S. leaders led them to conclude that the Soviets would certainly realize the seriousness of their actions, and would believe and heed the seriousness of President Kennedy's warnings about the missiles.

The crisis also illustrated that almost all forms of intelligence collection can have serious diplomatic consequences if compromised. Had a U-2 been shot down over Cuba without gaining clear evidence of the Soviet missiles, it would have been a major embarrassment to the United States, both internationally and domestically. The President must take into account the concerns of the State Department as well as the Intelligence Community in deciding how much risk is worth taking to gain the information needed to make wise policy in dangerous situations. There is no silver bullet formula for use in weighing the policy options in such scenarios. But it is clear that the potential danger to our national security of allowing Soviet missiles with nuclear warheads to be established secretly in Cuba warranted great diplomatic risks.

Another sometimes dangerous mind-set illustrated by the crisis is the general tendency of intelligence analysts and policymakers to give greater credence to electronic and photographic intelligence than to human source intelligence. This tendency has been exacerbated by the need within the intelligence community to protect the individuals and tradecraft involved in espionage, thus making intelligence leaders reluctant to release beyond a very narrow circle information about the source(s) of human intelligence. This, in turn, has made it difficult for analysts and policymakers to weigh the credibility of the information. Put simply, electronic and photographic intelligence is comparatively "hard" and thus comparatively easy to evaluate and use, whereas human intelligence is more problematic. Nonetheless, threats to our national security can often only be fully and timely understood by conducting espionage against our adversaries. Today information collected by espionage and counterespionage operations is shared more widely within the intelligence community, particularly with the Director of National Intelligence (DNI) and the DNI analytical components. The objective is to help the DNI evaluate more realistically the importance and accuracy of such information.

We must increase our capability to conduct all source intelligence collection operations against governments and organizations that pose a risk to our national security. This includes close cooperation with allied intelligence services. Espionage has been, and always will be, an important source of information for our security. To support our future national defense, it is essential that our government and our nation develop a better understanding of the long-term necessity to conduct espionage and other clandestine operations, and that our analysts learn how to give appropriate weight and credence to such intelligence. There will never be enough information from espionage agents, certainly not in the same quantity as intelligence acquired from technical platforms. Analysts must look at espionage as a vital but limited means of acquiring critical intelligence. You cannot turn espionage off and on like you can with technical collection assets. We should follow through on the commitment of outgoing President George Bush to increase our capability for HUMINT/Espionage by 50 percent.

The American operations officers who recruit and run these clandestine operations do so often at considerable risk to their own safety and the safety of their families overseas. It is essential that we as a nation develop a better appreciation for the integrity, skill, dedication, and courage of the men and women of America's National Clandestine Service. It is for this purpose and to these men and women that this monograph is dedicated.

ENDNOTES

1. Jerrold L. Schecter and Peter Deriabin, *The Spy Who Saved the World*, New York: Charles Scribner's Sons, 1992, p. 46.

2. *Ibid.*, pp. 43, 44, 46.

3. See *Ibid.*, p. 14, for the full name and translation of the GRU. Also see *Ibid.*, chap. 3, pp. 46-65. In 1965, the aforementioned committee was renamed the State Committee for Science and Technology.

4. *Ibid.*, pp. 204-205, 222-223, 346-350.

5. The above two paragraphs are from Mary S. McAuliffe and the CIA History Staff, *Cuban Missile Crisis, CIA Documents*, Washington, DC: Central Intelligence Agency, October 1992, pp. 139-145; Schecter and Deriabin, pp. 334, 351-352.

6. Schecter and Deriabin, summary of chaps 3, 10, 11, and 16.

7. Aleksandr Fursenko and Timothey Naftali, *One Hell of a Gamble. The Secret History of the Cuban Missile Crisis*, New York and London, UK: W. W. Norton & Company, 1997, p. 184n3.

8. The above three paragraphs are from Schecter and Deriabin, pp. 180-184, 222-224, 232, 330; Christopher Andrew and Oleg Gordievsky, *KGB – The Inside Story*, London, UK: Hodder and Stoughton Ltd., 1990, pp. 470-473. Note: Both of these books refer to Bolshakov as a KGB officer, but subsequent documentary information has shown that he was, in fact, a GRU officer. See Fursenko and Naftali, pp. 184, n3; 252, n30.)

9. Schecter and Deriabin, pp. 180-183; and the author.

10. Donald Kagan, *On the Origins of War*, New York: Doubleday, 1995. pp. 463, 466.

11. *Ibid.*, p. 476.

12. Andrew and Gordievsky, p. 469.

13. Kagan, p. 456; and the author.

14. Kagan, p. 476.

15. *Sherman Kent and The Board Of National Estimates, Collected Essays By Sherman Kent*, Sherman Kent and Donald P. Steury, eds., Washington, DC: Central Intelligence Agency, Center for the Study Of Intelligence, 1994, pp. 173-174; and the author.

16. See Schecter and Derabin, pp. 273-280.

17. *Ibid.*

18. *Ibid.*

19. *Ibid.*, p. 276; and the author.

20. Schecter and Deriabin, pp. 278-279.

21. *Ibid.*

22. Above two paragraphs from the author; Schecter and Deriabin, pp. 279-280.

23. Richard Helms with William Hood, *A Look Over My*

Shoulder, New York, Random House, 2003, p. 216.

24. Schecter and Deriabin, pp. 351-352.

25. This paragraph is from the author. Historians can also undervalue intelligence from espionage. Donald Kagan, in his 1995 book *On the Origins of War*, ignores the above memo from Proctor as well as the transcripts of clandestine meetings with Penkovsky, all of which were declassified by the CIA and published by Schecter and Deriabin in 1992. Kagan erroneously states that Penkovsky's information supported the inflated Soviet ICBM numbers. Quite the contrary, Penkovsky's information accurately contradicted the inflated numbers that were in the June 1961 NIE. Kagan, p. 490; and the author. See Annex C for discussion of intelligence sources used by the Soviets and the United States during the missile crisis and for definitions of clandestine operations.

26. Kagan, pp. 478-479.

27. Schecter and Deriabin, p. 226.

28. *Ibid.*, p. 280.

29. *Ibid.*, pp. 271-273.

30. Kagan, pp. 448-449.

31. Christopher Andrew, *For the President's Eyes Only*, New York: Harpercollins, 1995, pp. 275-276; Sam Halpern, Lecture To JMIC, April 15, 1998. Mr. Halpern was the executive officer to the Chief of Task Force "W," which was the CIA's Cuban Task Force during the missile crisis. I am indebted to the late Mr. Halpern for his editing of this paper on several subsequent occasions.

32. Helms, pp. 196-197, 200-203, 206-207.

33. The above four paragraphs are from *ibid.*; and Dino A. Brugioni, *Eyeball To Eyeball – The Inside Story of the Cuban Missile Crisis*, New York: Random House, 1991, p. 215.

34. Andrew and Gordievsky, p. 468.

35. General Anatoli I. Gribkov, Seminar at the Woodrow Wilson Center in Washington, DC, May 4, 1994, covered by C-Span 2.

36. *Ibid.*

37. Author.

38. Gribkov, Seminar; Fusenko and Naftali, p. 186; Schecter and Deriabin, pp. 68, 79, 100, 112, 140, 150, 266.

39. Gribkov, Seminar; Fusenko and Naftali, pp. 187-188.

40. Nikita Khrushchev, *Khrushchev Remembers*, Strobe Talbott, trans. and ed., Boston, MA, and Toronto, Canada: Little, Brown and Company, 1970, pp. 491, 493, 494.

41. The author; Khrushchev, *Khrushchev Remembers*, p. 493.

42. Above two paragraphs from Khrushchev, *Khrushchev Remembers*, p. 499; Nikita Khrushchev, *Khrushchev Remembers – The Last Testament*, Strobe Talbott, trans. and ed., Boston, MA, and Toronto, Canada: Little, Brown and Company, 1974, p. 511; and the author's recollection.

43. John Mack Faragher *et al.*, *Out of Many – A History of the American People*, Upper Saddle River, NJ: Prentice Hall, 2nd Ed., 1997, pp. 892-893.

44. Khrushchev, *Khrushchev Remembers*, p. 493; Khrushchev, *Khrushchev Remembers – The Last Testament*, p. 511.

45. The above four paragraphs are from Fursenko and Naftali, pp. 188-189. Also see General Anatoli I. Gribkov and General William Y. Smith, *Operation Anadyr – U.S. and Soviet Generals Recount The Cuban Missile Crisis*, Chicago, Berlin, Tokyo and Moscow: Edition Q, Inc., 1994, p. 4, for information on the FKR.

46. The above two paragraphs are from Schecter and Deriabin, pp. 312 and 412; Andrew and Gordievsky, p. 475.

47. Brugioni, pp. 72-73.

48. McAuliffe, p. 7.

49. The above two paragraphs are from James H. Hansen, "Soviet Deception in the Cuban Missile Crisis," Unclassified Article, *Studies In Intelligence*, Vol. 46, No. 1., Washington, DC: Central Intelligence Agency, 2002; and from the author's personal recollection.

50. Schecter and Deriabin, pp. 225, 319.

51. McAuliffe, p. 13.

52. Schecter and Deriabin, p. 331, p. 466n 13, and p. 466n 14; Author Interview with McCone, August 28, 1988.

53. Schecter and Deriabin, p. 331, 466n 14; Author Interview with McCone, August 29, 1988.

54. Above infomation on DCI McCone's warnings during August 10, 17, 21, and 23 meetings and his two memoranda to the President on August 10 and 22 are also contained in a memorandum for the record from McCone dated October 31, 1962. See McAuliffe, pp. 13-17.

55. The above two paragraphs are from the interview with McCone, August 29 1988; Schecter and Deriabin, pp. 331 and 466n 15.

56. Schecter and Deriabin, p. 332-333; Andrew, *For the President's Eyes Only*, pp. 282-284.

57. McAuliffe, pp. 35-37, 45.

58. *Ibid.*, pp. 40, 71. FKR cruise missiles were discussed earlier.

59. Schecter and Deriabin, pp. 325.

60. Robert F. Kennedy, *Thirteen Days — A Memoir of the Cuban Missile Crisis*, New York: W. W. Norton, 1st Ed., 1969, pp. 25-26; and Schecter and Deriabin, p. 330.

61. McAuliffe, p. 55.

62. Schecter and Deriabin, pp. 319-321.

63. *Ibid.*, pp. 325-327.

64. The above two paragraphs are from Fursenko and Naftali, pp. 211-212. See also Gribkov and Smith, pp. 4-7.

65. The above data on the Soviet build-up are from McAuliffe, pp. 7-8.

66. Above two paragraphs are from *ibid.*, pp. 39-98. Also see Schecter and Deriabin, pp. 332 and 333. The R-101 aircraft was used in low-level reconnaissance.

67. Schecter and Deriabin, p. 332.

68. Halpern and McAuliffe, pp. 364-365.

69. Brugioni, pp. 135-137.

70. *Ibid.*, note to reader on p. xi; Douglas F. Garthoff, *Directors Of Central Intelligence As Leaders of the U.S. Intelligence Community 1946-2005*, Washington, DC: Central Intelligence Agency, Center For The Study Of Intelligence, 2005, p. 32.

71. Brugioni, pp. 136-138.

72. *Ibid.*, pp. 139-140.

73. *Ibid.*, pp. 144, 151-152, 158-159, 165-167.

74. Kennedy, pp. 163-164. See President Kennedy's public address on October 22, 1962.

75. Brugioni, p. 144; McAuliffe, pp. 92-93.

76. Kent was the professor in full charge of the class, and he was not afraid to use salty language to make his point. He was an Ivy Leaguer who usually wore a loud necktie with the knot loosened below an open shirt collar, and who chewed tobacco in class. Kent earned a Ph.D. in history from Yale, and taught at Yale prior to World War II. During the war, he worked in the Research and Analysis Branch of the Office of Strategic Service (OSS), becoming chief of the Branch's Europe-Africa Division.

77. The above two paragraphs are from author's recollection; and Kent and Steury, Introduction, p. x.

78. The author; and Brugioni, pp. 144-145.

79. Kent and Steury, p. 179.

80. The author.

81. Brugioni, pp. 144-145; McAuliffe, pp. 1-3; and the author.

82. Author's recollections and opinion, p. 62.

83. A. Denis Clift, *Clift Notes: Intelligence and the Nation's Security*, 2nd Ed., James S. Major, ed., Washington, DC: Joint Military Intelligence College (JMIC), August 2002, p. 17. In December 2006, the JMIC was re-named the National Defense Intelligence College.

84. Brugioni, pp. 159-160.

85. *Ibid.*, p. 160.

86. *Ibid.*, p. 160 and 215; McAuliffe, pp. 103-104.

87. Author's opinion; Brugioni, p. 105.

88. The above two paragraphs from Schecter and Deriabin, pp. 330-331.

89. The above two paragraphs are from a declassified memo from McCone, October 11, 1962; McAuliffe, pp. 123-125.

90. The above two paragraphs from McAuliffe, pp. 366-370.

91. McAuliffe p. 139-145, Schecter and Deriabin, p. 334.

92. McAuliffe, p. 105; and the author.

93. The above two paragraphs from the author, and McAuliffe, pp. 107-108.

94. McAuliffe, p. 103-104.

95. Brugioni, pp. 164-165, 181.

96. Helms, pp. 213-215.

97. *Ibid.*, p. 216.

98. Max Holland, "The 'Photo Gap' That Delayed Discovery of Missiles in Cuba," Unclassified Article, *Studies In Intelligence*, Vol. 49, No. 4, Washington, DC: Central Intelligence Agency, 2005; and the author.

99. The author.

100. Brugioni, p. 208.

101. *Ibid.*, p. 239.

102. Kagan, pp. 507-508.

103. Brugioni, pp. 239-240.

104. McAuliffe, p. 245; Brugioni, pp. 336-338.

105. Brugioni, p. 232.

106. *Ibid.*, p. 234-237, p. 251.

107. McAuliffe, pp. xv, 159-160, 169-173; and the author's recollection. A special information channel using code

word "Psalm" was established to restrict the dissemination of information concerning Soviet missiles in Cuba.

108. McAuliffe, pp. 167-168.

109. Kennedy, pp. 40-41; and the author.

110. Above two paragraphs from McAuliffe, pp. 197-202.

111. *Ibid.*, pp. 203-208; and the author.

112. For the above three paragraphs, see McAuliffe, pp. 211-220.

113. *Ibid.*, pp. 159, 237; and the author.

114. Kennedy, pp. 37-38, 47-48; Brugioni, p. 315; Ernest R. May and Philip D. Zelikov, *The Kennedy Tapes. Inside the White House During the Cuban Missile Crisis*, Cambridge, MA, and London, UK: The Belknap Press Of Harvard University Press, 1997, pp. 191-193.

115. The above four paragraphs are from May and Zelikov, pp. 189-203.

116. The above three paragraphs are from the memorandum from McCone giving his account of this meeting. See McAuliffe, pp. 241-242.

117. Memorandum on McCone's briefing of Eisenhower, see *ibid.*, pp. 243-244.

118. McCone's memorandum, see *ibid.*, p. 245.

119. The above paragraph is from Andrew, *For the President's Eyes Only*, pp. 292-293; also Brugioni, p. 332.

120. Author's recollection. For a list of other diplomatic steps taken by the U.S. State Department during October 20-22, 1962, see May and Zelikov, pp. 214-215.

121. Andrew, *For the President's Eyes Only*, pp. 294; Kennedy, pp. 53-55; and Brugioni, p. 363.

122. Kennedy, pp. 163-171; and from the author. It was ironic that on the same day President Kennedy made his speech to the nation, Colonel Penkovsky was reportedly arrested in Moscow. His arrest was not announced publicly until *Pravda* did so on December 12, 1962.

123. *Ibid.*

124. Halpern Lecture. See also Brugioni, pp. 366-367.

125. Brugioni, pp. 367.

126. Brugioni, pp. 75 and 265, Stephen E. Ambrose with Richard H. Immerman, *Ike's Spies*, Garden City, NY: Doubleday and Co., 1981, p. 85; and the author.

127. Brugioni, pp. 366-368.

128. *Ibid.*, pp. 371, 409-410.

129. Author, p. 63.

130. Kennedy, pp. 57, 60.

131. Halpern.

132. Brugioni, p. 391.

133. *Ibid.*, pp. 398, 400-401.

134. *Ibid.*, p. 401.

135. Andrew, *For the President's Eyes Only*, p. 297.

136. Excerpt from CIA memorandum, "The Crisis, USSR/ Cuba," October 24 1962. See McAuliffe, pp. 295-296.

137. Brugioni, p. 423.

138. Excerpt from CIA memorandum, "Crisis, USSR/ Cuba." See McAuliffe, pp. 303-304; Brugioni, pp. 423-424.

139. Andrew, *For the President's Eyes Only*, p. 298.

140. Kennedy, pp. 81-83.

141. Andrew, *For the President's Eyes Only*, p. 299.

142. Fursenko and Naftali, pp. 271-274; Kennedy, pp. 97-99; Gribkov and Smith, p. 7.

143. Kennedy, pp. 15-16, 101-104; May and Zelikov, pp. 560, 603-604.

144. Above two paragraphs from the author's recollection; and McAuliffe, pp. 9-12.

145. The author's recollection.

146. For Joint Evaluation of Soviet Missile Threat in Cuba, see McAuliffe, pp. 323-325.

147. The above two paragraphs from Kennedy, pp. 107-109.

148. The above two paragraphs are from the CIA memorandum. See McAuliffe, pp. 341-343.

149. Kennedy, p. 110.

150. Andrew, *For the President's Eyes Only*, p. 302-308; Halpern from personal recollection.

151. Schecter and Deriabin, pp. 337-348.

152. *Ibid.*, pp. 346-350.

153. Fursenko and Naftali, pp. 309-313.

154. The above two paragraphs from the CIA memorandum; see McAuliffe, pp. 357-360.

155. Above two paragraphs from Brugioni, pp. 543, 546-548.

156. Clift, pp. 30-32.

157. *Ibid.*, pp. 32-33.

158. The above six paragraphs are from McAuliffe, pp. 362-371; and the author.

159. Memorandum, McGeorge Bundy to Evelyn Lincoln, March 7, 1963, "Killian, James R. 2/4-3/7/63" folder, President's Office Files, Special Correspondence, Box 31, JFKL. President's Foreign Intelligence Advisory Board, March 11, 1963. Memorandum for the file: "March 8 and 9 Meeting of the PFIAB." Assassination Records Review Board, Record 206-10001-10012, p. 1; and the author.

160. McAuliffe, p. 366.

161. *Ibid.*, pp. 367-368.

162. *Ibid.*

163. *Ibid.*, pp. 367-369.

164. *Ibid.*, pp. 361-371.

165. Kennedy, p. 111.

166. *Ibid.*, pp. 14, 127-128.

167. Above two paragraphs from Schecter and Deriabin, p. 336; Helms, p. 216; and the author.

168. *Ibid.*

169. Andrew and Gordievsky, pp. 477-478.

BIBLIOGRAPHY

Stephen E. Ambrose with Richard H. Immerman, *Ike's Spies*. (Garden City, NY: Doubleday and Co., 1981.)

Christopher Andrew, *For the President's Eyes Only*. (New York: Harpercollins, 1995.)

Christopher Andrew and Oleg Gordievsky, *KGB – The Inside Story*. (London, UK: Hodder and Stoughton Ltd., 1990.)

Dino A. Brugioni, *Eyeball To Eyeball – The Inside Story of the Cuban Missile Crisis*. (New York: Random House, 1991.)

Denis Clift, James S. Major, ed., *Clift Notes: Intelligence and The Nation's Security*, 2nd Ed. (Washington, DC: Joint Military Intelligence College, August 2002.) Mr. Clift was president of the JMIC, a part of DIA, in 2002. He is currently president of JMIC which in December 2006 was renamed the National Defense Intelligence College.

John Mack Faragher, Mari Jo Buhle, Daniel Czitrom, and Susan H. Armitage, *Out of Many – A History of the American People*. (Upper Saddle River, NJ: Prentice Hall, 2nd Ed., 1997.)

Aleksandr Fursenko and Timothey Naftali, *One Hell of a Gamble. The Secret History of the Cuban Missile Crisis*. (New York and London, UK: W. W. Norton & Company, 1997.)

Douglas F. Garthoff, *Directors Of Central Intelligence As Leaders of the U.S. Intelligence Community, 1946-2005*. (Washington, DC: Central Intelligence Agency, Center For The Study Of Intelligence, 2005.)

General Anatoli I. Gribkov and General William Y. Smith, *Operation Anadyr – U.S. and Soviet Generals Recount The Cuban Missile Crisis*. (Chicago, Berlin, Tokyo and Moscow: Edition Q, Inc., 1994.)

Sam Halpern, Lecture To JMIC, April 15, 1998. Mr. Halpern was the executive officer to the Chief of Task Force "W," which was the CIA's Cuban Task Force during the missile crisis. I am indebted to the late Mr. Halpern for his editing of this paper on several subsequent occasions.

James H. Hansen, "Soviet Deception in the Cuban Missile Crisis." Unclassified Article, *Studies In Intelligence*, Vol. 46, No. 1. (Washington, DC: Central Intelligence Agency, 2002.)

Richard Helms with William Hood, *A Look Over My Shoulder.* (New York, Random House, 2003).

Max Holland, "The 'Photo Gap' that Delayed Discovery of Missiles in Cuba," Unclassified Article, *Studies In Intelligence*, Vol. 49, No. 4. (Washington, DC: Central Intelligence Agency, 2005.)

Donald Kagan, *On the Origins of War.* (New York: Doubleday, 1995.)

Robert F. Kennedy, *Thirteen Days — A Memoir of the Cuban Missile Crisis.* (New York: W.W. Norton, 1st Ed., 1969.)

Sherman Kent, Donald P. Steury, ed., *Sherman Kent and The Board Of National Estimates, Collected Essays By Sherman Kent.* Washington, DC: Central Intelligence Agency, Center for the Study Of Intelligence, 1994.)

Nikita Khrushchev, Introduction, Commentary, and Notes by Edward Crankshaw, Strobe Talbott, trans. and ed., *Khrushchev Remembers.* (Boston, MA, and Toronto, Canada: Little, Brown and Company, 1970.)

Nikita Khrushchev, Introduction by Jerrold L. Schecter; Foreword by Edward Crankshaw; Strobe Talbott, trans. and ed., *Khrushchev Remembers — The Last Testament.* (Boston, MA, and Toronto, Canada: Little, Brown and Company, 1974.)

Ernest R. May and Philip D. Zelikow, *The Kennedy Tapes. Inside the White House During the Cuban Missile Crisis.* (Cambridge, MA, and London, UK: The Belknap Press Of Harvard University Press, 1997.)

Mary S. McAuliffe and the CIA History Staff, *Cuban Missile Crisis, the CIA Documents*. (Washington, DC: Central Intelligence Agency, October 1992.)

Jerrold L. Schecter and Peter Deriabin, *The Spy Who Saved the World*. (New York: Charles Scribner's Sons, 1992.)

ABOUT THE AUTHOR

KENNETH MICHAEL ABSHER currently is a Fellow with the Scowcroft Institute of International Affairs, the Bush School of Government and Public Service, at Texas A&M University. He retired from the Central Intelligence Agency (CIA) as a member of the Senior Intelligence Service, having served over 31 years in the clandestine service. Mr. Absher was Chief of Station in two different field assignments, and Chief of Base in two others. He had four tours in CIA Headquarters managing foreign intelligence operations. Mr. Absher also served in Western Europe, the Caribbean, and Indochina. He provided direct intelligence support to the U.S. handling of major Cold War events such as the 1962 Cuban Missile Crisis, the Vietnam War, the 1983 military and rescue operation in Grenada (Operation URGENT FURY), and the break-up of the Soviet Union and the Warsaw Pact. Mr. Absher has taught at the University of Texas at San Antonio, and from 1997 to 2002 at the Joint Military Intelligence College (now known as the National Defense Intelligence College) in Washington, DC. From January 2003 to February 2005, Mr. Absher served on the Joint Terrorism Task Force in San Antonio, Texas. During 2005, Secretary of State Condoleezza Rice appointed Mr. Absher as the DCI representative to three Accountability Review Boards to investigate terrorist attacks in Iraq. Mr. Absher graduated from Phillips Exeter Academy and holds a B.A. in Philosophy from Princeton University.

ANNEX A

THE OFFICE OF NATIONAL ESTIMATES[1]

The predecessor of the Office of National Estimates (ONE) was the Office of Reports and Estimates (ORE), which was part of the new the CIA created by the National Security Act of 1947. After the ORE failed to foresee the North Korean invasion of South Korea on June 25, 1950, President Truman chose Lieutenant General Walter Bedell Smith to replace Admiral Roscoe Hillenkoetter as the DCI. In November 1950, Smith brought Harvard diplomatic historian William L. Langer and Yale historian Sherman Kent into the CIA. Both were veteran analysts of the Office of Strategic Services (OSS), which was the U.S. clandestine foreign intelligence and paramilitary service during World War II. ORE was then replaced by the new ONE. Henceforth, NIEs were to be produced by a Board of National Estimates, which was a part of the ONE. Langer became the head of the ONE and Chairman of the Board of National Estimates, with Kent as his deputy. After Langer returned to Harvard in 1952, Kent took over both positions where he remained until he retired on December 29, 1967, after more than 30 years of government service.

During the 1960s, the IC expanded in size and capabilities. In 1961, the Defense Intelligence Agency (DIA) was created. In 1973, DCI William Colby abolished ONE. He replaced it with a system of National Intelligence Officers which exists today, known as the National Intelligence Council.

1. Donald P. Steury, "Introduction," Donald P. Steury, ed., *Sherman Kent and the Board of National Estimates, Collected Essays by Sherman Kent*, Washington, DC: Central Intelligence Agency, Center for the Study of Intelligence, 1994, pp. xi, xii, xxiv.

ANNEX B

THE UNITED STATES INTELLIGENCE BOARD

The U.S. Intelligence Board (USIB) was created by President Eisenhower by National Security Council Intelligence Directive (NSCID) 1, issued in April 1958 and reissued in September that same year, to account for the creation of the new USIB. Eisenhower had a strong desire to force greater integration in the American IC. This new NSCID 1 gave the DCI an explicit formal mandate "to coordinate the foreign intelligence effort of the United States, in accordance with the principles established by statute and pertinent National Security Council directives." This was an even stronger formulation than was contained in the 1947 National Security Act. Yet the DCI at the time, Allen Dulles, continued to urge and persuade rather than force management of the intelligence community. Eisenhower backed off and accepted Dulles' collegial style of management rather than replace him.[1]

The USIB was initially comprised of 12 persons with mixed backgrounds: academics, retired diplomats, senior military officers, business executives, and lawyers. Once an NIE had been drafted and reviewed by the Board of National Estimates, it was submitted to the USIB which was comprised of representatives from all of the members of the Intelligence Community. The USIB was chaired by the DCI in his role as the leader of the Intelligence Community. Once an estimate was approved by the USIB, the DCI then had the responsibility to disseminate it to the White House and to the National Security Council.[2]

In the opening sentence of the January 16, 1962, memorandum from President Kennedy to the new

DCI John McCone, the President said that "In carrying out your newly assigned duties as Director of Central Intelligence, it is my wish that . . . you undertake, as an integral part of your responsibility, the coordination and effective guidance of the total United States Foreign Intelligence effort." Unlike Dulles, McCone enthusiastically welcomed his role as community leader. He particularly wanted to enhance the nation's intelligence capabilities by applying modern science and technology. The President's memo instructed McCone to work closely with the "heads of all departments and agencies having responsibilities in the foreign intelligence field." This meant that the DCI outranked the other intelligence chiefs, and was expected to deal directly with their superiors. The President also said that he expected the DCI would delegate much of the task of running the CIA to the Deputy Director of Central Intelligence (DDCI), permitting him to focus on his "primary task as Director of Central Intelligence."[3]

Until January 1962, the DCI presided as Chairman of the USIB and acted as the CIA representative on the USIB. Based on the President's memo, McCone decided that he could be more impartial if he served as Chairman of the USIB with the DDCI serving as the CIA representative on the Board. McCone did this to emphasize his role as a broad leader of the American IC, not necessarily tied to the CIA positions. To improve even further his ability to guide and manage the intelligence community, McCone considered separating himself entirely from the direct management of the CIA. Although this would also have been in line with President Kennedy's memorandum, McCone was not able to implement this additional step. Moreover, during the missile crisis, McCone further decided that he could not serve as chairman of the USIB while simultaneously functioning as a member of the EXCOM. He asked DDCI General Carter to chair the USIB during the crisis.[4]

ENDNOTES

1. Douglas F. Garthoff, *Directors of Central Intelligence as Leaders of the U.S. Intelligence Community, 1946-2005*, Washington, DC: Central Intelligence Agency, Center for the Study of Intelligence, 2005, pp. 34–36.

2. Richard Helms, with William Hood, *A Look Over My Shoulder*, New York: Random House, 2003, pp. 234-235.

3. Garthoff, pp. 41-42, 48.

4. *Ibid.*; Dino A. Brugioni, *Eyeball To Eyeball – The Inside Story Of The Cuban Missile Crisis*, New York: Random House, 1991, p. 283.

ANNEX C

MAJOR INTELLIGENCE SOURCES USED DURING THE CRISIS

Soviet Intelligence Sources.[1]

SIGINT - (GRU telephone intercepts in Washington).

KGB penetration of NSA and U.S. Embassy in Moscow.

"Sasha" - U.S. military intelligence officer recruited by the KGB in Germany in 1959. He was stationed in Washington during the Cuban Missile Crisis in 1962, but could only supply low level intelligence during the crisis.

U.S. Intelligence Sources.

Penkovsky - Soviet GRU officer who provided the CIA and British MI-6 with voluminous intelligence beginning in April 1961, but who lost his access to senior Soviet military officers in July 1962 just when we needed this access the most. Our last operational contact with him was August 27, 1962, at a reception in the apartment of the American Agricultural Attaché in Moscow. Documents were clandestinely exchanged. He was sighted again on September 5 at an American embassy reception; and on September 6 at a British film showing. His arrest was announced on December 12, 1962. Penkovsky was tried, and his execution was announced in May 1963.[2]

U-2 photos – After U-2 flights resumed over the interior of Cuba on October 14, 1962, this photography in "triangulation" with Corona photos of missile sites in the USSR, and manuals for the SS-4 and SS-5 missiles which were provided by Penkovsky's espionage gave the U.S. excellent intelligence coverage of the status of missile site construction and readiness.

NSA SIGINT

CIA espionage agents in Cuba.

Cuban refugee debriefings - some 1,500 to 2,000 Cuban refugees were debriefed every week in Miami.

Clandestine Operations.[3]

The *Clandestine Service* within the CIA conducts espionage, counterespionage and covert action. It was initially known as the Directorate of Plans. It was subsequently renamed the Directorate of Operations. It is now known as the National Clandestine Service and is under the direction of the DCIA.

Espionage is still not understood by many persons in government, journalism and academe. Espionage is the clandestine collection of information about the plans, intentions, and activities of foreign governments, organizations, and persons, by human or technical means. Human espionage involves the recruiting, training and running in place of an agent who serves and reports to us as a clandestine source. Espionage conducted by technical means is not the collection of intelligence by overt platforms such as aircraft and satellites. An example of espionage by technical means would be the clandestine installation of an audio device in a conference room used by senior officials of a foreign government.

Counterespionage is the clandestine collection of information by human or technical means about the plans, intentions, and activities of foreign governments, organizations, and persons to conduct espionage, sabotage, assassination, and acts of terrorism. Counterespionage operations may also be operations designed to counter or protect against espionage, sabotage, assassination, and terrorism—not just to collect information.

Covert action is a third category of clandestine operations. It is designed to influence foreign governments, events, organizations, or persons in support of U.S. policy objectives. Covert action operations are normally conducted in a manner to conceal the identity of, or to permit plausible denial by the sponsor. Such operations may include political, economic, propaganda, or paramilitary activities.

ENDNOTES

1. Christopher Andrew and Oleg Gordievsky, *KGB – The Inside Story*, London, UK: Hodder and Stoughton Ltd., 1990, pp. 475-476.

2. Jerrold L. Schecter and Peter Deriabin, *The Spy Who Saved the World*, New York: Charles Scribner's Sons, Macmillan Publishing Company, 1992, pp. 351-352.

3. Kenneth Michael Absher, *Defining Intelligence*, Washington, DC: Joint Military Intelligence College (renamed the National Defense Intelligence College), March 2002.